PUBLIC RELATIONS IN THE MARKETING MIX

Introducing
Vulnerability Relations

PUBLIC RELATIONS IN THE MARKETING MIX

Introducing
Vulnerability Relations

Jordan Goldman

NTC Business Books
a division of *NTC Publishing Group* • Lincolnwood, Illinois USA

1995 Printing

Published by NTC Business Books, a division of NTC Publishing Group,
4255 West Touhy Avenue, Lincolnwood (Chicago), Illinois 60646-1975 U.S.A.
Library of Congress Catalog Card Number: 83-71076

4 5 6 7 8 9 0 VP 9 8 7 6 5 4

To Elaine, Todd,
and Marc

Table of Contents

Acknowledgments

The origins of this book reach back to my earliest school days when I first became aware of and privy to my father's deep insights into marketing. So my first debt of gratitude is to my dad, who I still believe was years ahead of his time.

My thanks, too, to Ron Greenstone and Ken Rabasca of Greenstone & Rabasca Advertising for giving me free rein to practice public relations in the broad-brush ways described in this book.

And, of course, thanks to my wife, son, and daughter for their forebearance during my many, many hours at the typewriter and while I was rummaging through dust-covered account files in the basement of my home for recollections of strategies covered in these pages.

Introduction

Although this book is about public relations, it is primarily concerned with PR as a *marketing*—not as a *management*—tool. The publics with which it deals are not internal—officers and employees—but external: Customers, suppliers, and distributors. And the means of communications that it employs are usually not bulletins, newsletters, and annual reports but the media and more or less public events. While all public relations is concerned with strategy, *marketing-oriented* PR is concerned with *marketing* strategy—with the development of means and ends directly related to buying and selling.

Two Types of Public Relations

PR marketing strategy can be divided into two broad areas of activity. The first, which is largely dictated by company marketing objectives, seeks to publicize the company and its products or services. Reflecting the company's sales goals, choice of markets, and positioning, this type of PR strategy is offensive rather than defensive, opportunity-seeking rather than problem-solving, and "proactive" rather than "reactive." Even though it deals with current and near-term change, proactive PR is nevertheless guided by long-term marketing policy. This is so partly because the changes with which it deals reflect internal influences—that is, company decisions, plans, and programs. Therefore, they are foreseeable, if not entirely controllable. In addition, such changes are positive. That is, they do not involve problems; instead, they offer opportunities. And, therefore, the policy governing their PR treatment can be relatively straightforward and simple. The question is not *what* to do, but *how* to do it. If the news is good, for example, it should be publicized. The only issue is: What medium or event should be used to publicize it?

The second area of marketing-oriented public relations is determined by outside influences—usually changes in the marketplace. Because most such changes—in government policy, consumer attitudes, or competitive actions—are not company- instigated, they cannot be planned for. They are usually not governed by marketing policy. And, therefore, they must be dealt with on an ad hoc basis. They require a decision as to *what* to do, as well as *how* to do it. Furthermore, the changes with which reactive PR deals are usually negative. They are problems to be solved, rather than opportunities to be taken, and they require defensive, rather than offensive, measures. Unlike proactive PR, which tries to enhance the company's image and increase its revenues, reactive PR tries to restore the company to the status quo—by repairing its reputation, preventing market erosion, and regaining lost sales.

So important is this reactive form of public relations (and so often overlooked as a marketing tool) that it is probably worthwhile to give it a name of its own. Since proactive PR deals with a company's strengths and reactive PR deals with a company's weaknesses, we could call the latter "vulnerability relations"—or "VR"—to distinguish it from its somewhat older and more well-established cousin.

The proactive form of PR is traditionally employed in dealing with company goals and achievements: Gaining product exposure; announcing company, corporate, and personnel changes; disclosing news related to company finances and well-being; and publicizing state-of-the-art engineering developments.

Even these few functions embrace more than many companies regard as the scope of PR. In otherwise sophisticated firms, PR is often relegated to an infrequent news release about product or personnel. In many instances, there is little understanding of the nuances of the press release and even less of the ways PR can be used strategically. For example, the difference in psychological impact between an article by-lined by a company executive and one written by the publication's staff often escapes even experienced marketers.

Reactive PR has been a neglected topic in public relations partly because its strategic value in marketing is not well understood, and partly because it is less easily planned for than proactive PR. Not only are the occasions on which it is needed frequently unforeseeable, but the strategies that it requires are varied. The typical reactive PR situation often demands a far more complex response than does proactive PR.

First, if the PR problem is based on an actual weakness or shortcoming, then initial efforts must be aimed internally at company management, urging it to solve the problem. Then PR strategies must be targeted at the company's external publics, informing them that the problem has been or is being solved. What makes the PR response even more complex is the need to avoid a straightfoward denial that the problem exists. Because no company wants to call attention to its problems, it must handle them indirectly. Therefore, reactive PR must deal somewhat circumspectly with its external publics—and sometimes with the media—purporting to say or do one thing while it is actually saying or doing another.

Negative publicity about a company or its product may arise accidentally or fortuitously, or it may result from deliberate actions by competitors—in which case PR must be directed at other companies, as well as external publics. This negative publicity may be based on weaknesses or shortcomings that are alleged but not actual. When that is the case (and it frequently is), then the PR program must not only seek to discover the source of the allegations and stop them, but also convince external publics that the charges are false.

In the chapters that follow, we'll approach public relations from several points of view. One of these will cater to the needs of the PR novice who is just getting started. He or she may be taking college communications courses or may be switching to public relations from some other field. We'll also approach PR from the point of view of the journalist-turned-PR-person. He or she may have broad writing, reportorial, and media expertise, yet may be inexperienced in marketing and marketing communications. We'll also be addressing the professional PR practitioner whose career has been concerned largely with management-oriented PR and little with marketing-oriented PR. Experienced in the skills of communications, he or she may nevertheless be unaware of PR strategies that can be used to address marketing-type situations. Then there is the corporate executive who needs to understand more fully how marketing-oriented PR can benefit his company. And, finally, we'll be addressing the PR professional who is currently involved in marketing-type communications activities, yet is interested in adding to his or her storehouse of strategic PR weaponry.

In considering the needs of these varied readers, our discussion will cover the problems of choosing PR vehicles, determining what kinds of PR a company needs, ferreting out problem situations, writing a PR plan and presenting it convincingly to management, and developing strategies for dealing with a variety of marketing situations. In terms of this last area, we'll be dealing largely with vulnerabilities—how they affect relationships with the public and how they can be overcome.

In part one of this book, on proactive PR, we will discuss a variety of PR techniques and the situations in which they can be used. We will focus on the opportunities for using PR as a finely tuned marketing communications vehicle. The strategies discussed, addressing themselves to a host of problems, provide marketing leverage often unattainable through traditional communications approaches.

Some of the techniques we'll be examining offer the "little voice" a chance to be heard. They enable companies that may be wanting in certain strengths to succeed, regardless, in the marketing arena. Davids can often take on Goliaths. New or smaller companies can compete, head on, with entrenched competitors.

The second part of this book, on reactive PR, deals with situations in which a company—because of its products, its people, or some other facet of its operation—is somehow placed in an underdog position. As we'll see, that underdog position can have a telling effect on sales and can undercut the many positive things a company may have going for it.

Techniques discussed here also enable a company to engage in the throwing of little punches—what might be called "infighting." Scarcely an organization exists that doesn't occasionally have regional or local brushfires affecting some facet of its operation. Yet few companies can afford advertising dollars for stamping them out, even though such problems might wipe out a territory. Many of the procedures covered here offer effective, low-budget approaches for just such occasions.

PR as a Marketing Tool

Most important of all is that marketing strategy as discussed in this book is addressed from the PR point of view, providing a blueprint that virtually anyone can follow, experienced or not in marketing. PR procedures are described for accomplishing strategic goals which, in many instances, are more effective and powerful than traditional marketing approaches. And they are described in such a way that management can readily see the vital role PR can play in the marketing communications mix.

Of course, management's understanding of the potential value of public relations is indispensable. It is impossible to recount how often this publicist, together with ad agency executives, has sat in on meetings with new agency clients who hadn't yet finalized their marketing communications budgets. It was often appalling, after listening to their marketing problems, to see them forego powerful PR remedies that stood excellent chances for success while they proceeded unquestioningly with the ad program.

In many instances, these companies were in desperate need of the PR approach as an adjunct to their advertising. Yet management hadn't the foggiest notion of PR's strategic potential. Many managers were unaware that advertising might not be able to accomplish everything by itself—that certain marketing situations can, in fact, neutralize what advertising tries to accomplish and that these same situations can be handled effectively and economically through PR.

It would be an understatement, indeed, to say that marketing has come a long way in the last few decades. That the world will beat a path to our door for a better product is no longer an acceptable premise. What marketing people have learned over the years is that no sales can be made if the public is not convinced that the product or service offers some advantage. And sales can rarely be made if the public is not reassured that the company marketing the product or service is reliable, financially sound, and well managed.

In spite of the sophistication that marketing tools have attained, however, they are not always effective. Some marketing programs do not succeed because they are under-budgeted. Yet, even some programs with seemingly unlimited budgets do not increase sales. Why? Often, well-funded and well-designed marketing efforts fail because the company lacks credibility. An audience that doubts the sincerity of a message may opt for the competitor's product. And the realization of this problem has made public relations—often used for other purposes—a valued tool for marketing. Overcoming the "credibility gap" always has been one of public relation's strong suits, usually through "third-party" endorsement. (The third party may be an editor, reporter, or satisfied customer.)

The ability of third-party endorsements to lend credibility to a company's sales message can best be understood by comparing publicity with advertising. The latter is, of course, paid for by the advertiser. Within certain limits, the advertiser can say pretty much what he chooses about his product. Knowing that, those who are exposed to advertising—readers, TV viewers, etc.—will believe the claims if they have some reason to trust the advertiser or if they know that a particular advertising medium will not sanction unsubstantiated claims.

By and large, however, the public tends to believe that once a company plunks down its advertising dollars with a certain publisher or broadcast medium, it can claim whatever it wants. That belief, whether true or not, certainly diminishes the credibility of the advertising message.

In contrast, the public puts greater stock in what appears in the media in the form of editorial material. Unlike advertising, it hasn't been paid for by the advertiser. Should an editor, columnist, or TV personality choose editorially to applaud a product, service, or company, the chances are excellent that whatever he says will be believed.

Therein lies a major benefit in having marketing-oriented public relations run concurrently with advertising. Once the public is satisfied with the credibility of a claim through editorial comment, the advertising message will gain in credibility, too.

Because of that simple fact, more and more marketing people are realizing that public relations is a powerful tool to be used either by itself or in conjunction with advertising. As a result of its credibility, it helps induce the world to beat a path to a company's (or dealer's) doorstep. But it also does something else. *It extends the "reach" of advertising.* Few companies can afford to have their ads reach out to more than their primary markets. Nor can they afford to run their ads in more publications than is absolutely necessary. (Complex studies are often undertaken to screen out media overlap and audience duplication, because it wastes advertising dollars.) And publications that are not judged the very best in reaching a particular market will often get scratched when communications budgets shrink.

Publicity, on the other hand, because of its cost-effectiveness, can be directed at virtually *all* appropriate media—both primary and secondary. And the more overlap, the better the impact. The cost of a few extra press releases or postage stamps is negligible compared with the cost of running ads in those additional media. If the information in the release is appropriate for the medium's audience, there is a good chance the editor will use it—without charge. Of course, the message may get edited or incorporated into some larger article. But it's still exposure. And it's free. There is a good possibility, too, that the message will get picked up by a wide range of media, thereby lengthening the reach of the advertising program for very few additional dollars. It may also gain exposure for the company in many more markets—just for a few extra cents in postage. And when the advertising budget is not big enough to embrace some of the other products in a line, PR is a way to obtain exposure for them at negligible expense.

The marketing man, however, should not regard public relations as simply a way to save dollars. Some PR vehicles cost every bit as much as advertising. For example, a company might want to do a motion picture film about itself and distribute it to theaters, schools, and civic organizations. That kind of public relations doesn't come cheap. It does, however, offer a certain touch—possibly its credibility—that cannot be duplicated by other communications vehicles. Then the dollars invested may well be justified.

Public relations communications can even appear as ads, carrying messages that do not mention a product or service but bolster a company's image or argue a particular company position to influence congressmen or voters. In such instances, the cost of advertising must certainly be reckoned with.

Credibility, low cost, extended reach in the same markets, and exposure in additional markets are some of the reasons for using PR to get a message across. Greater credibility is justification in itself for using PR. And it need not be confined to claims about a product or service. Extra credibility may be needed to bolster claims about a company or its practices that are of concern to its various publics (e.g., customers, vendors, or shareholders). That is an extremely important function of PR, which this book will treat at length.

Part One

PROACTIVE PR

1

Developing a PR Program

Basically, developing a PR program is simply a method of thinking ahead. Based on marketing objectives, planning should result in a long-term program of proactive PR activities. The program should provide a schedule for handling more or less predictable and controllable PR opportunities, such as new product introductions and plant expansions. And it should provide guidelines for dealing with the unforeseeable but—in the course of a year—inevitable changes, such as personnel promotions. The program should delineate step-by-step procedures for using the techniques of PR—alone or in conjunction with advertising or other forms of communication. Without a program, PR efforts are likely to be unfocused and uncoordinated. As such, they are unlikely to accomplish marketing objectives.

A PR program, then, should involve some kind of written document on which everyone can agree. Agreement is important because it often makes the difference between a plan's success or failure. Many PR (and advertising) practitioners can reel off story after story about how, after months of implementing a program for a company, they were suddenly confronted by management with a question, "What are you doing and why are you doing it?"

Getting management to agree initially on objectives, general strategy, and even specific actions saves considerable frustration later on. That in itself is reason enough to have a written plan that management can consider and ultimately approve. Then, after the plan has been initiated, no one can claim he was not aware of it.

The PR Audit

However, before you put a PR plan into writing, you must arrive at the strategy behind it.

To formulate a PR strategy, it's important to start by interrogating the people directly involved with it—presumably, the marketing and sales executives. Although it is best to get input from as many of them as possible, it is essential to get as much information as you can from the marketing director.

What kind of information should you expect from such an interrogation? Essentially, the data derived from a PR audit are much the same as that needed to develop advertising strategy. For the sake of efficiency, the heads of both advertising and PR departments or executives from the ad and PR agencies can interrogate a company's marketing management simultaneously. (The session is referred to as a "communications audit.") Both will be interested in pretty much the same material.

To obtain as much information as possible from the audit, it's best to prepare in advance a typed questionnaire, copies of which the company's marketing people and the communications professionals can refer to together. The questionnaire pries loose basic information, which usually leads to even more questions, providing still deeper insight into marketing situations. Varying widely in their coverage, some questionnaires are extremely lengthy, running for pages and covering every last shred of detail about a company, its people, its publics, its vendors, and its investor relationships. Yet, some are quite brief, covering only the essentials. The PR practitioner must decide how long the questionnaires should be, based on how much information he needs in order to produce an effective plan.

Here's a quick look at items that might appear on the questionnaire.

For openers, knowing whether the company is private or public helps to determine what kinds of information can, should, or must be given media exposure. For example, if a company is public, it must meet certain Securities and Exchange Commission (SEC) disclosure requirements. This means that any information that might conceivably affect the rise or fall of stock prices must be reported immediately. Quarterly and annual reports—also within the domain of the PR practitioner—must be prepared and distributed to shareholders. When a company is privately held, such information can be withheld or disclosed, depending on the particular marketing advantage each bestows on the company.

Information on the divisions of the company and what they produce or what functions they perform should be requested on the questionnaire. Even if the PR program is just for one division, reference to other divisions in a feature article or some other PR vehicle can be strategically valuable.

The audit should also elicit information on the products produced by the various divisions in order to determine which products are to receive PR emphasis. Specific details about the products, unless essential to the PR strategy, can be filled in at a later meeting.

Market penetration and relative profitability of each product are important facts to know in developing a plan. They can help determine how much PR effort should be allocated to each product.

The competition for each product is vital information. No strategy can be conceived in a vacuum. Knowledge of who the competition is, what it is doing to gain or hold market share, how its products perform in the marketplace, and how they are perceived there (e.g., expensive, well designed, good quality, etc.) are all grist for the PR mill.

Other essential audit items are:

Company goals for each product. This includes, among other things, expected sales increases in the near and long terms, geographic distribution goals, and the product's anticipated increase or decrease in importance to the company.

Market trends for each product. This will include a recent history of the product, its markets, and its competition—and anticipation of future trends. Such information can, for example, help determine whether an educational program is needed prior to a program aimed primarily at sales.

New product introductions. This includes whether similar and competitive products already exist, their relative merits, and their potential markets.

Reputation of the company among competitors, vendors, customers, and shareholders. (This is important information, but probably difficult to obtain.)

Plants, branches, research, and manufacturing facilities. This information can be used in company backgrounders, articles, or news releases.

Significant achievements of the company and its executives provides additional strategic input.

Important customers. This information can result in valuable case-history material for future articles.

The list can go on and on, depending on how much information you need and how much management is willing to convey to you. (Busy executives might say "enough" when you start reaching areas they feel will little influence what *they* consider relevant to a PR program.)

Other items on the questionnaire might be:

- Channels of distribution
- Warehousing
- Delivery of product (positive and negative aspects)
- Existing patents
- Membership in associations
- Participation in trade shows
- Product weaknesses
- Pricing
- Packaging (positive and negative aspects)
- Purchasing influences (direct and indirect)
- Seasonality
- Export markets
- New markets
- Advertising thrusts
- Important dealers
- Noteworthy in-store tie-ins
- Methods of handling promotion-generated leads
- Sales and marketing problems

Once all this information has been accumulated at the audit, the PR and advertising people can begin their individual formulations of strategy. These strategies can (and in many instances should) dovetail. When ad and PR professionals are under one roof, as in an ad agency with a public relations division, it is not unusual for both plans to be presented to the client as a single entity with separate ad and PR sections.

Writing a PR Plan

Let's turn now to the writing of the PR plan (the strategy in written form), which will be presented to company management.

There are two opposing views on the appropriate length of written plans. One holds that brevity is essential, partly because (it is assumed) nobody will read more than two or three pages. The other view contends that comprehensiveness is essential because management, to be fully convinced of the program's merits, must see all i's dotted and t's crossed. Such a PR plan can run on and on until all bases are covered. Perhaps the best solution to this dilemma is to straddle the two approaches. Both a short and long version of the plan can be packaged together in a single binder. Of course, which version is best depends to a great extent on whom the PR practitioner must convince.

The abbreviated version of the plan is actually an outline. The lengthier version covers not only the details of the program but also its rationale and ramifications. It is written with the assumption that whoever reads the plan will want to understand fully how each facet works—and why.

Whatever its form, the PR plan ought to include certain basic elements. It should make maximum use of the information unearthed at the audit. By doing so, it shows management that the audit session was not just window dressing and meant solely to impress; it gives management an opportunity to correct any mistaken notions or incorrect facts conveyed during the audit; and it reassures management that the PR plan is based on information derived from the audit and that it is not a standardized, universal plan that will fit any company in any situation.

CURRENT SITUATION

The section presenting audit-derived information normally comes at the beginning of the plan. It can be labeled "current situation"—or something to that effect. Of course, this section can be broken down further into "domestic" and "foreign" or "internal" and "external" categories.

Because this section of the plan is nothing more than an organized presentation of management-originated information, management needn't read it thoroughly and carefully, except to correct errors. The information can be given in outline form, with clipped, outline-style phrases. Full sentences needn't be used except where meaning might be blurred, and topics can be listed and flagged by bullets (asterisks or dots).

PROGRAM OBJECTIVES

Once the "current situation" has been described, "program objectives" can be presented. This section should be keyed to items in the first section. It can be subdivided into "immediate" and "long range" categories. This section is important because it provides management with an opportunity to see that the program consists of *numerous* intermediate objectives. Left to itself, management would more than likely state a solitary, ultimate objective, such as "increasing sales" or "increasing profits," with no hint of what steps must be taken to achieve these objectives. Proper assessment of a PR program's value hinges directly on management's realization that intermediate objectives *do* exist. Intermediate objectives may be enumerated in outline form or listed and bulleted. A typical objectives list might read as follows:

- Heighten credibility of product benefits
- Increase product exposure in trade media
- Elevate stature of R&D department
- Provide distributor in Cleveland with media exposure in its immediate market area
- Gain exposure in investor-oriented media
- Develop press kits for three trade shows
- Organize press conference to introduce new widget in September
- Provide sales organization with publicity reprint material for sales call leave-behinds
- Generate inquiries
- Support advertising campaign

As you can see, intermediate objectives are bite-size steps leading to the ultimate "increase profits" objective. In other words, they denote areas that the PR program can address individually. And program success can be measured by assessing progress with respect to each objective. However, it should be emphasized that the actual achievement cannot be anticipated by marketing or other company executives. What they should expect, instead, is that the PR program will move the company closer to attaining the objectives. Like the pitcher in a baseball game, the PR director depends on the efforts of the rest of the team. And if he or she fails, the fault might lie elsewhere.

It bears repeating that dependence on company management for establishing PR objectives is a mistake. As we've noted, management tends to oversimplify them. Besides, management should not be expected to be as conversant with the possible achievements of a PR program as the public relations practitioner. Relying on management for formulating objectives might result in a PR program labeled a failure when, in reality, it might be successfully accomplishing exactly what it was (realistically) expected to do.

RATIONALE

Following (or even preceding) the "objectives" portion of the plan, it is important to state unequivocally, in however many words it takes, why the PR approach is recommended at all. Company management might feel that it is adequately promoting itself or its products—without PR. It is the purpose of this portion of the plan to point out what PR can be expected to achieve over and above the company's other efforts. Now is the time to talk about PR's cost-effectiveness, its ability to extend the reach of advertising, its power in increasing the credibility of the sales message, its use as an inexpensive way of discovering new markets or of measuring interest in a new product, its ability to generate leads, its usefulness in prescreening advertising media, and so on.

If PR is truly warranted, then this section of the plan— whether it is a paragraph, a page, or several pages—must be strong enough to convince management of it. No matter how large a company may be, it does not want to waste money that might otherwise be spent on higher priority projects. Besides, it is not universally assumed that PR is an essential ingredient of the marketing mix. This is the time to roll out the big guns and make sure that the arguments for the PR are heard.

VEHICLES

The intermediate portion of the plan—the section that comes before the closing statements—should deal with the PR program itself—the vehicles to be used and their functions. If the plan is more than an outline, then the arguments for each type of vehicle should be fully presented, possibly with suggested topics for releases and articles. How all this fits into the overall strategy should be included.

This section should be divided into subunits, each of which has a heading that briefly sums up its contents. The portion dealing with press releases, for example, might simply be designated "Press Release Program." Under that heading would come all the arguments and examples needed to convince management of the value of press releases, including topics covered by the releases.

Separate subunits might be labeled "Press Kit," "Feature Article Program," "Seminars," "Merchandising the Publicity," "Generating Inquiries," "Establishing Leadership," "Addressing the Financial Community," etc.

Selling the Plan

In all this, it is important to bear in mind that the PR professional is supposed to be the member of the marketing team who is most knowledgeable in matters of PR. He plays the role of PR advisor or counselor to company management. Consequently, it is expected that he will do a little "educating" in his PR plan—not simply describing a particular PR vehicle but giving full arguments as to *why* the vehicle should be used at all. Too often, crucial segments of a PR plan are excised by a company executive because he does not fully understand their relevance to the program as a whole. Convincing him and others of strategies that the PR practitioner knows by experience to be effective frequently requires the publicist to play the role of salesman. PR people who are able to produce convincing arguments on paper, as well as in face-to-face encounters with management, will have fewer of their plans dismembered.

Because of their detail, plans tend to lose some amount of forcefulness by the final page. This happens because the reader finds it hard to keep in mind all of the "convincers" sprinkled throughout the plan. This, coupled with an abrupt close after the final subunit, increases the risk that the plan will finish on a "down" note, devoid of emotional impact.

If the plan is to succeed in convincing management, its emotional appeal must be restored. The place to do this is in the closing paragraph, reiterating *briefly* the elements to be included in the program and the explanations of their importance. Handled skillfully, the final paragraph of the plan should have the reader eager to get on with the program.

It may seem that invoking the techniques of salesmanship removes the element of professionalism from PR. But this is not the case. Everyone is skilled in his own area and expected to know more about it than others do. When the PR practitioner genuinely believes that what he is recommending is important to the marketing of a product or service, it is his duty to convince management of that. Anything less should make the publicist feel that he has failed to present his case as well as he could have.

The PR practitioner, then, must be ready to defend his recommendations, sharpening whatever skills are necessary to do it, whether it involves forceful writing, face-to-face confrontation with management, or a formal stand-up presentation.

Re-audits and Supplementary Plans

Simply because a plan has been written doesn't mean it is cast in concrete. Markets change continually, as do product lines, competition, financial situations—and even companies. For a PR program to be effective, it must reflect these changes. For that reason, marketing communications audits should be conducted periodically—possibly once a year. But waiting for company management to request an audit might mean a long wait, indeed. Not totally conversant with PR (at least to the degree that a PR practitioner is), management might fail to recognize how certain changes in the company's situation can affect the PR program. Depending on the industry, one audit a year might be too few or too many. But once a re-audit is done, a revised plan which takes recent changes into account, should be drawn up. That plan, too, must be "sold" to management—with the same conviction as the original one.

Supplementary plans should also be generated whenever the

publicist is called on to put an unusually large effort into one specific facet of the overall program. A press conference, for example, might merit a plan of its own. Without it, non-PR executives could fail to grasp the detail work and strategizing involved in such a media event. Details for a press conference can take months to implement, possibly requiring slide presentations, speech and press-kit writing, site selection, stage settings, badges for participants and guests, catering arrangements, invitations, and so on. A plan specially drafted for that event should spell out reasons for staging the press conference (as opposed to other ways of accomplishing the same objective). It should cover activities that precede and follow the event and should include a timetable or flowchart that shows when each element will be initiated, approved by client or management, put into production and completed, and when invitations will be sent out. In short, every last detail *and* rationale for the event ought to be covered in the plan.

Implementing the Plan

Experienced PR practitioners can attest to the fact that company management often contributes unwittingly to a program's mediocrity—even its demise. It happens in a most unexpected way, as the following scenario will demonstrate.

Program slippage or failure often begins right at the start of the program. Thanks to the convincing arguments offered in the plan, company management is enthusiastic about it and decides to work closely with the PR team. So far, so good. It is precisely this kind of management involvement that strategic PR needs. It enables the PR executive to be privy to management's thoughts and marketing problems.

However, when everything is running smoothly, management begins to feel that, with the program going so well, it no longer has to work closely with and oversee the PR people. This is the beginning of the end. When the feeling is strong enough, management withdraws and turns the program over to a coordinator, who inherits near-total responsibility for it. From that moment on— unless the coordinator is thoroughly experienced in PR and understands every aspect of the PR plan—the program goes downhill.

The PR team finds itself increasingly isolated from management, its thoughts, and its problems.

Lacking these critical management inputs, the program usually degenerates until it becomes simplistic, nonstrategic and ineffective, contributing little to creative marketing communications strategy. Once on the downside of the curve and falling fast, the program eventually falls into disfavor with management, which finds that the money budgeted for it can be better allocated elsewhere.

The moral of the story is: Don't let it happen. The way to avoid it is to keep management involved, primarily by maintaining contacts with upper echelon executives as often as possible, while resisting attempts at transferring the program to any but executives who are knowledgeable and experienced in marketing communications.

Fortunately, not all PR programs follow that fatal scenario. But PR practitioners must constantly be on their guard against it. Regardless of the PR team's good intentions and the program's merits, it will pass into mediocrity and possibly dissolve entirely, unless management involvement is maintained. This is a peculiarity of truly strategic PR—it depends on the kind and quality of inputs that only high-level company executives can provide. When these inputs are obtained, PR can become one of the most powerful strategic weapons in a company's marketing arsenal. But when the information faucet is turned off, PR is left swimming in an empty pool.

The success of a PR program also often depends on the level of PR counsel involvement. Although strategic PR rests heavily on management inputs, non-PR executives should not decide which PR situations demand PR activity. However, in order to maintain the proper involvement for making such decisions, PR people cannot be removed from the intimate goings-on within a company and brought in only when management feels like it. That, in effect, leaves the calling of PR shots to nonprofessionals and virtually destroys the tremendous potential of strategic marketing PR.

The way to remedy such a situation is for the PR professional to be involved continually—not merely on a project-by-project basis. He must bear the responsibility for counseling management

365 days of the year. That way he won't surface solely at the discretion of non-PR types and possibly miss out on opportunities that may well have warranted PR treatment.

Besides turning publicists into permanent members of a company's marketing team, this approach goes a long way toward upgrading the status of a company's internal PR staff. It transforms sometime PR people into full-time professionals. More than that, it assures management that PR will be utilized to its fullest potential in furthering marketing objectives.

2

The Product Release

Now that we have explored the development of the PR program, it is time to examine its implementation. Although we shall discuss only the most common PR vehicles in the next few chapters, it should not be assumed that there are no others. By combining necessity and creativity, practitioners can always develop new strategies, invent new techniques, and discover new vehicles.

One of the most frequently used PR vehicles is the press release, which is simply a communication of company news to the public through the media. It can be used to publicize new products, report on company achievements, and announce personnel changes. Relatively easy to draft and to disseminate, it is a multifunction vehicle that can be used in a variety of situations and for a variety of purposes.

The product release, one form of the press release, is essentially what its name implies. It is a brief announcement of news about a product or service. It describes the features of the product, emphasizes its benefits or uses, and (possibly) indicates its price. The product release also tells how additional information can be obtained.

The product release usually follows a standard format. It begins with a brief heading, normally in upper-case type, which indicates, in one or two lines, the product's primary features or benefits. Secondary product characteristics may be stated directly beneath the headline in a single subhead, usually in upper- and lower-case type.

The headline should be "paid off," or elucidated, in the first one or two paragraphs. Someone lured into reading the item because of the headline must find it frustrating if the subject of the headline is not discussed immediately.

The remaining paragraphs of the release are used to elaborate on the opening couple of paragraphs. Or they may be used to introduce additional, but less important, features. The next-to-last paragraph includes a mailing address, a phone number, and tells how to order the product or get more information. The final paragraph, known as the corporate paragraph, briefly describes the company, its other products, its markets, and—if important—its size, growth, or leadership in the field.

Publicizing Products

The most common function of the product release is to support the advertising program. In this respect, it is a flexible PR vehicle because it can be used to reach several different audiences or one particular audience. Furthermore, especially compared to advertising, the product release communicates cheaply and efficiently. The cost is limited to running off multiple copies, reproducing photos, and postage. And it can be carefully targeted to almost any market.

However, perhaps the most important advantage of the product release is that, because of its low cost, it can be used again and again—not only in a great variety of media, but repeatedly in the same media. Too often, the target media are limited to the few publications used in the company's small budget advertising program. But such arbitrary restraints on distribution result in the underuse of a powerful vehicle that can greatly extend the reach of advertising. The product release should be directed at the broadest conceivable array of media—especially to reach audiences that cannot be reached in any other way.

In addition, this important PR vehicle should not be bound by the "one-product, one-release" rule. Because almost every product has more than one feature, benefit, and application, it can sustain a series of releases, each one devoted to a particular product characteristic. This fact enables the PR practitioner to develop a long-term release program for every product and enables the company—even with a limited product line—to keep its name before the public on a continuing basis.

PRODUCT FEATURE RELEASE

The need to keep a steady stream of releases flowing is not widely appreciated. And the methods of doing so are not generally understood. This was the case, for example, with the manufacturer of a limited line of timing devices. The company wanted to develop a promotion program capable of generating large quantities of leads. Its sales representatives were eager to get this kind of assistance. Yet, the company's advertising, constrained by a tight budget, was too small to give much help.

Fearful of losing its rep organization for lack of much-needed assistance in tracking down prospective buyers, the company nevertheless could find no way out of its dilemma. It executives felt that the product line was too small for product publicity to be of any help—although they realized that product releases frequently produce volumes of sales leads. The firm's executives were strapped by the traditional "one-product, one-release" concept. But such an approach would do little to augment the firm's meager advertising exposure. After issuing one release for each of its few products, what then? Back to the same trickle of leads from the scanty ad program?

Fortunately, however, through the counseling of an outside PR firm, the company discovered it could count on product releases to do much more than its marketing executives had imagined.

That timing device company isn't alone in its misconception of product release usage. Considered by many to be a cut-and-dried vehicle, it actually lends itself to a multitude of strategic uses that often are completely overlooked in a marketing communications program. Examining the timer manufacturer's revised approach provides some interesting insights into the versatility of this PR vehicle.

What originally would have been the only release about one of the products in the company's line turned out, instead, to be just the first in a series of releases on the product. How was that accomplished?

The first release announced the product's key features in the headline and echoed them in greater detail in the opening paragraphs. With each succeeding paragraph, the release expounded an addition features and benefits—in increasing detail. That would have been the end of the PR campaign for the product had the company's marketing team not recognized that some customers might want their product for reasons quite different from those that the team supposed. Applying that recognition, they began to view the product release in an entirely different light—one that acknowledged that different product features appeal to different markets.

In the case of the timing device, some prospective customers might have been attracted by its ability to function under water. Others might have been interested in its operational temperature range. However, both pieces of information were buried somewhere towards the end of the first release, and they probably failed to attract the attention of at least some prospects who might have been interested in them.

The first release listed an entire array of features, any one of which might have warranted an inquiry from the field. In the new approach, the company produced a series of releases, each of which elevated one feature to a position of prominence in the headline and opening paragraphs. This meant that two, three, or more totally different releases were written for each product—each heralding a different feature.

PRODUCT APPLICATION RELEASE

Another approach to multiple versions of the product release is based on product applications. In addition to different features, the timing device had different applications, and each application provided an opportunity for a separate release. Of course, in this case, the application (not the feature) became the main issue. The headline announced that a timer was available for a specific purpose (e.g., timing the spray cycle for a drive-in automated car wash). Again, the initial paragraphs supported the headline, and succeeding paragraphs showed how the timer's construction made the application possible.

Applications are not as easy to come by as are product features, which can be taken directly from the product specification sheet or the manufacturer's catalogue. If the product is new, all of its applications may not be known. After it has been marketed, however, the manufacturer need only consult the sales staff about past and present applications. If the product is sold through distributors or reps, the manufacturer must ask them how the product is being applied. The timer company, for example, checked regularly with its reps on how their customers were using the timing devices. A company can obtain this information by mailing reminders to reps or distributors or by directing its internal sales staff to collect the information during phone conversations or meetings with customers. Still another way is to provide the PR staff with a list of sales organization contacts. Then, whenever they need information, PR people can pick up the phone and get it directly from a rep or a distributor.

MINI-CASE-HISTORY RELEASE

A kissing cousin of the product applications release is the mini-case-history. The chief difference between them is that end-user names do not appear in the former but are used prominently in the latter.

Of course, a mini-case-history usually would not appear in a publication's product section. Similar to a full-length case-history feature article—but in abbreviated form—the "mini' would probably appear in the "application briefs" section of a publication (called by a variety of names in different magazines).

In addition to giving the user's name, a mini-case-history should explain why the product was selected (e.g., what problems it solved) and mention its benefits (e.g., flexibility, reliability). As with a case-history feature article, the manufacturer must obtain permission (preferably in writing) from the end-user about whom the release is written.

The chief difference (other than length) between the case-history feature article and the mini-case-history release is that the former is generally submitted to a publication on an exclusive basis. That is, the company agrees not to offer it to competing publications (or, in some cases, to any other publication at all). Like any other product release, the mini-case-history release can be mailed to a broad media list, unencumbered by such restrictions. Theoretically, it can appear in dozens—even hundreds—of publications.

The mini-case-history and the feature or application release do not go to the same editor. The latter should be addressed to the "product editor." This is important because few editors take the time to reroute a release that doesn't pertain to their department. It's easier for them to ignore it. Since all publications do not have the same designation for editors or departments, it is a good idea to play it safe and address the mini-case-history release to the "editor." That way, it will find its way to the person designated to receive incoming editorial matter not specifically addressed to any one person or department.

SCREENING LEADS

Product releases can generate unbelievable quantities of leads. However, it is sometimes alleged that the quality of the leads is not particularly good. That is, the people who inquire may not be very interested in buying. Inquiries might come from literature collectors, who just want to keep their files bulging, and time-servers, who want to look busy and do so by reading material in which they have no real interest.

The problem is simple. Not knowing the quality of the leads supplied by their company, salespeople call on these supposedly potential customers. But because these respondents are indifferent to the product, the salespeople end up wasting their valuable time. And the experience is demoralizing.

Two consequences can ensue. First, the salespeople may become suspicious of all the leads supplied by the home office—to the point of refusing to follow them up. As a result, the value of the entire product release program is nullified.

Second, the sales force may become disillusioned with the company itself. After all, the sales job might have been appealing solely or largely because the company promised to supply dependable leads. Should they be found wanting, all the time and effort spent on assembling a good sales organization will have been wasted. The salespeople will simply take off for companies with more reliable leads.

However, there is no need to risk demoralizing or losing the sales organization. There is a way to be reasonably sure that the leads supplied by product releases are dependable: Prescreen the leads.

A very effective method of prescreening leads is to double-qualify them. This is not a new idea, but it can make all the difference to people who are responsible for producing high-quality leads. Double-qualifying means that the potential customer is asked to indicate his interest in the product at least twice.

Getting the prospect to respond twice accomplishes something very important. It makes him demonstrate that he has more than just a passing interest in the product. How the manufacturer goes about making the prospect respond twice is definitely an art form. Properly done, however, it can prove beyond doubt that the prospect is actually in the market for the product.

But doing it *properly* is the critical element. If the manufacturer merely has a clerk call the prospect to verify his address or title or mails him a card asking him to respecify what literature he wants, the results may be of no greater value than the original response.

However, if the company responds to the prospect's inquiry by getting him to stipulate specifically what his problem is or why he is interested in the product, the second response on the part of the prospect will be much more reliable.

The material sent out to elicit the second response should require a little thought and time on the part of the prospect. It can consist simply of a question or two. Better still, it can be a full-blown questionnaire asking him to clearly define his need for the product. Anyone who responds to that type of inquiry and expresses a legitimate need for the product is at least genuinely interested in hearing more about it. Of course, whether or not he buys depends largely on the product and the sales rep. But double-qualifying leads gives them both a chance to do their job.

The first step in guaranteeing reliable leads to the sales force —whether generated by publicity or advertising—is, therefore, to withhold initial responses from the salespeople. Meanwhile, a questionnaire should be ready to be mailed instantly to the prospect. Then, when the prospect submits his second response, the filled-out questionnaire should be sent to the appropriate salesperson. Once a sales organization receives these second responses, it should have no qualms about following them up. In fact, a sales force supplied with double-qualified leads will welcome them and look forward to receiving them.

Attracting Customers

Until now, we have considered only manufacturers of products aimed at industrial-type audiences. But what has been said applies equally to companies marketing consumer-oriented products or services.

Let's examine the case of a pantryware manufacturer with national distribution—in both department and housewares stores—but a relatively small advertising budget. Many companies had become competitive with it, offering a similar line of pantryware items—particularly canisters for coffee, flour, sugar, and tea; cake servers; breadboxes; and step-on refuse cans—all in matching sets.

With competition growing, the firm had to increase its level of consumer media exposure. That, it was hoped, would help convince retailers to keep the company's items on their shelves. Consumer publicity—augmenting the company's limited national advertising, while not significantly increasing its communications budget—seemed the best means of achieving these objectives.

However, like that of the timer manufacturer, the company's line was small. Using just the traditional product release (one product, one release) the line could have generated only half a dozen releases—not enough to gain media exposure sufficiently continuous to draw new customers into the stores. For this reason, the pantryware manufacturer decided to distribute a variety of releases over a period of years.

A MODEL RELEASE PROGRAM

An important feature of the canisters made by the company was that they nested together compactly when not in use. That feature prompted a how-to release on achieving more counter space in the kitchen. Because the release touched on kitchen items other than the canisters, it didn't sound like an out-and-out plug for the product. And it provided hints for organizing items on countertops. Although well disguised, the canister plug was in there, nevertheless. Yet, the release sounded very much like the kind of advice a home editor would give to family-page readers. A photo of the canisters, accompanying the release, showed them in a kitchen setting. Not simply a photo of the product alone, it illustrated the points made in the text.

Pickup of that release by the media was quite good. Major newspapers throughout the country were the main target. Others were Sunday supplements; syndicated columnists specializing in home-making; shelter magazines, such as *House and Garden;* women's magazines, such as *Ladies' Home Journal;* and farm and rural publications that cover family life, such as *Grit.*

Another release about the canisters discussed arranging the kitchen to cut down on wasted footsteps. It pointed out the advantages of having sugar and flour canisters nearby when needed. Of course, besides indicating where the canisters should be placed, the release recommended what type of canisters to purchase so as to conserve limited counter space. The release buried the plug for the canisters in surrounding material that provided suggestions on working efficiencies totally unrelated to canisters.

Still another release required a lot of research but resulted in numerous and quite satisfying media pickups. It showed the historical evolution of the canister, with photos of containers used by early American settlers, ultradecorative canisters used in the kitchens of royalty, and the modern-day canister set with *its* advantages —obviously the subject for which the company was seeking exposure.

One release showed how to decorate a kitchen so that appliances and countertop items do not clash. Naturally, an important role in the story was played by the canister set, photographed with specially colored enamel finishes and simulated wood-grained exteriors that matched the kitchen cabinets.

THE NEED FOR CREATIVITY

The media of choice for consumer items must, of course, be consumer-oriented: Newspapers (dailies and weeklies), general and specialty magazines, wire services, and syndicated columns. You must convince these major publicity outlets that the information in your release is worth printing. Needless to say, however, the competition for space in such media is fierce. You must compete with virtually every consumer-oriented company in the United States and elsewhere.

To get into print in consumer media, the product release must, therefore, provide the editor or columnist with something unusual and exciting. Consequently, an indispensable element in consumer product releases is creativity, which can be achieved in both style and content. The copy must be lively and concise. Although the subject can be treated humorously, melodramatically, or matter-of-factly, it must be treated consistently. The release can use a human-interest approach or a how-to angle. It can focus on an unusual aspect of the product. It can present statistics. And it should be accompanied by good photos or drawings to illustrate the main theme or idea.

If the release is creative enough, newspapers, wire services, and syndicates might use it—possibly just as it was sent to them. Or the release might convince a magazine to take its own photo of the product and write its own caption—which it might not have done had it not received your release.

As the case of the pantryware manufacturer shows, any number of releases can be written about any consumer-type product. And creative approaches are virtually unlimited. With editors constantly in search of a new and different angle, it is challenging to try to find one they like. Thus, despite the competition, it is best to keep trying new approaches until you strike a rich vein. Then you can mine it. And, after you've exhausted it, you can try digging somewhere else—creatively.

Testing Markets

The product release is usually regarded as a means of promoting a product that has been deemed marketable. However, it can also be used to determine whether a market for a new product actually exists.

Ascertaining marketability prior to expending large sums on advertising and promotion can be extremely valuable. Ordinarily, such information is obtained through focus groups and other well-established market research techniques. Although they are excellent tools, these testing methods present two problems. First, they are quite costly. They can eat up lots of money before any valid market analysis is completed. Second, they are not infallible. Even the use of several different techniques for testing a market does not produce certainty. Many products have tested well and yet failed miserably in the marketplace.

In this context, market testing by means of product releases offers two advantages. First, it allows the marketer to institute another method of analyzing the market. Second, it costs almost nothing. Thus, used in conjunction with more traditional market research techniques, it can at least add another measure of reassurance—relatively cheaply. And if your budget is such that the usual methods are too expensive to use at all, the product release can provide an inexpensive alternative for testing the waters.

Again, for little more than the cost of postage, a product photo, and the printing of the release, it is possible to determine in advance if favorable reaction to your product can be generated. Granted, the results will not be foolproof. But, whether used by itself or combined with other research methods, the product release can add a little certainty to a very uncertain situation.

In the product release approach, interest in the product is determined solely by the number of inquiries the release generates. Only a few inquiries might indicate a low interest level. Yet, products that are very costly (say, in the $50,000-and-up range) might require only a few interested prospects to turn the product into a rousing success.

Needless, to say, a new product tested in this manner should be either immediately deliverable or close to it. Testing the market in the hope of developing a product on the basis of the results would very likely alienate potential customers and hurt the company in the long run.

Of course, markets can also be tested for a fully developed, in-production product that is not only marketable, but is already being marketed. Such testing is necessary when a company decides to extend a product that is successful in its present markets into new markets. Here, too, the product release can be an important tool.

In this instance, however, the market-testing release can exploit the success that the product has already achieved. It can describe an in-use application. Or it can be written in the form of a mini-case-history.

Again, the level of interest in the new market is determined by the number of inquiries generated. And although a large number of inquiries does not guarantee success, at least it allows for even more information-gathering. Salespersons visiting or calling prospects can ascertain the perceived merits of the product, the need for it, and the nature and extent of the competition. In short, exposure of the release in a new market can open the door to a host of benefits for the company—at a cost that, by comparison with the benefits and the cost of other research techniques, is insignificant.

By now, it should be evident that there is a considerable amount to know about product releases, their uses, and the strategies connected with them. And considering their possibilities, it should be clear that relegating their development to a back-office function—having them cranked out by someone who is only minimally knowledgeable about public relations—is missing out on the tremendous potential of an extremely powerful and versatile PR vehicle.

3

The Executive-
Statement Release

The product release may be the most widely used PR vehicle, but
it is not the only one. In fact, it is unlikely that a PR program
depending exclusively on such releases will bear much fruit. At
the very least, it will fail to take advantage of the many strategies
and approaches that are available through the use of other PR
vehicles.

This is so primarily because the product isn't everything. That
is, considerably more is involved in the sale of a product than the
product itself. A simple case will illustrate.

Let's say that you need new roofing for your house, and you
must have it installed before you leave for your summer vacation.
Otherwise, the roof might leak while you are away and ruin your
furniture and carpeting. Here, you are unquestionably interested in
more than the product—in this case, the roofing material. Because
of the urgency of the problem and because you will be unable to
supervise the job, you are concerned about the reliability of the
contractor. You want to be sure that the work will be done by the
time you return—or sooner. In addition, you want to be certain
that the contractor won't substitute inferior materials. And you
want to ascertain whether he warrantees his workmanship for a
number of years.

If you are a careful buyer, you also want to be sure that the
contractor has access to a wide variety of roofing materials. And
you'd like to know whether he is able to maintain a sizable inventory—just in case his supplier goes on strike or goes out of
business before the job is completed.

Some of the assurances can be supplied by consulting friends and neighbors who have used the contractor and can vouch for his reliability. However, this isn't always possible, especially with a company that services a large geographical area and whose customers are far-flung and generally inaccessible. In this case—and the same point applies to all companies with national and even regional distribution—you must rely on some other source of information than direct, first-hand experience with the product. In fact, the assurance you need pertaining to the contractor's warrantee is almost totally unavailable by direct inquiry because it relates to the company's financial stability, its long-term manufacturing/marketing plans, and its vendor relationships.

So even in something as simple as having your house re-roofed, much more is involved than the roofing material. And the same is true of any important purchase. This is why marketing-oriented PR that is focused exclusively on the product is not particularly effective. A product-release campaign may attract a flock of inquiries. And a mini-case-history release may elicit interest, too. But the marketing of the product may never get beyond that point. The salespeople following up those leads may not be able to close many deals because something is missing from the PR program—namely, the assurances consumers need before they make a purchase.

Selling Reliability

The just–cited illustration raises three sales–related problems.

The first problem is that marketing almost never involves merely the matching of a product with a physiological need. It also involves matching a product idea with a more or less psychological need. In the case of the roofing contractor, for example, the real product is *reliability*. And the need it satisfies is *security*. To be sure, other products satisfy a wide variety of psychological needs—e.g., to be sexually appealing, to be fashionable, to be individualistic—but every product lives and dies on its reputation for delivering on its promises—for satisfying the need to feel secure and confident.

The second problem is that—except for very small or very large companies—there is no way of evaluating product or service reliability completely and definitively. The local mom-and-pop grocery store may be able to get people in the neighborhood to spread the word about the quality of its fruits and vegetables. The shoe repair shop may be able to rely on word-of-mouth for vaunting the dependability of its services. And high-ticket vendors may be sure that their customers will thoroughly investigate the reliability of the product before they buy, both through on-site inspection and interviews with customers. But for buyers of anything between metal washers used as a minor component in the manufacture of air conditioners, on the one hand, and automobiles, on the other, user verification is often either hard to come by or not worth the time and effort it would take to get it.

The third—and most important-problem is that the question of reliability *will be raised.* And it *will be answered,* whether the company tries to answer it or not. The potential customer will simply rely on his or her *sense* of the company's reliability. And, if this is uninfluenced by advertising or public relations, it may not be favorable to the company.

The solution to all three problems is simply to *sell* reliability —that is, to develop credibility for the company, focusing on non-product facets of the company's operation. It's difficult to establish such credibility through advertising because the advertiser purchases the publication space or broadcast time and thereby buys the right to say whatever he wants to say about himself or his product. For this reason, the only promotional messages that can successfully establish credibility are the ones that are presented through *third-party endorsement:* Editorial messages.

That is why a product release or a company-by-lined article— which may establish interest in the product—should not be expected to do very much in the way of building confidence in the company manufacturing or marketing the product. Naturally, the more product exposure, the better. It's a necessary ingredient in a sale. But it does little more than gain exposure for the product and possibly generate inquiries. All those other questions—about financial stability, relationships with vendors, ability to live up to delivery promises, and so on—also need to be answered to the prospect's satisfaction, *before* a sale is effected.

For that reason, a marketing-oriented PR program must make use of a variety of vehicles and approaches—not just the product-exposing type. These other vehicles help bolster those additional images of a company so that, in the end, the prospect will feel secure in purchasing the product or service.

What follows will show how various PR vehicles are used strategically to get across *convincingly* all those other issues that are really what a prospect must consider before settling on a specific purchase.

The Executive-Statement Strategy

In the marketing of a product or service, the image of a company as an industry leader—and of its executives as authorities in their field—plays an important role. In fact, establishing this imagery (as we've witnessed with the roofing material example) is just as important as establishing the quality of a product or service.

Like children playing ''follow-the-leader,'' companies and consumers tend to follow (or flock to) front-runners—companies that are considered progressive, dependable, or both. It is also considered ''safer'' to do business with such a leader. Since other people have found the company reliable, why not follow suit?

A leadership image has another distinct advantage: It can go a long way—as later chapters will point out—toward dispelling an underdog image that may plague a company just starting out, entering a new market, or suffering from a bad reputation.

In addition, the public generally finds it more comforting and less risky to do business with companies whose executives, engineers, or scientists are regarded as experts and authorities. The fact that they *are* authorities seems to augment the leadership image of the companies they work for. It is hard to conceive of people who are considered authorities being associated with organizations that are not, in their own right, significant forces in their industries.

How does a company get to be considered a leader in its industry. And how do its executives become known as authorities?

THE EXECUTIVE-STATEMENT RELEASE VS. THE PRODUCT RELEASE

Let's begin answering these questions by taking a look at a press release category quite different from that of the product release. It's the *executive-statement release*. And it's different for several reasons: It needn't discuss a product; it's written largely as a statement or quotation from a company executive; and it usually appears in a different section of the publication.

Consider that last difference first. The product release normally appears in the section of a publication reserved for products (frequently near or past the middle of the magazine). It's usually printed with other product writeups in a special section, where as with a shopping center, all sorts of different stores are grouped together to draw large numbers of potential customers. Like the shopping center, the product section draws readers shopping for new product ideas in one or several product categories.

The executive-statement release, on the other hand, does not belong in the product section. Instead, it fits most naturally in the news section—probably the most highly read part of any publication, be it consumer, trade, or industrial. Ask any magazine advertiser where he'd most like his ad to be positioned, and he'll probably say opposite or on the same page as the news. Virtually everyone interested in what's happening in a certain field turns to the news section. Being included there—rather than in the product section—carries with it a certain measure of prestige. Few clients of mine ever report back that their product publicity appearing in the "New Products" section evokes any great enthusiasm during a sales call or at a trade show. But get the smallest mention in the news section of a publication and their telephones start ringing, prospects bring it up at sales calls with some degree of awe, and industry peers let them know they've seen it.

· Consider this. Events that occur in or relate to a field or industry are what editors like to report on in their news columns. Usually these events consist of significant happenings that involve well-known companies, points of view of important industry executives, and governmental or environmental impacts on an industry. Whatever these news items may be about, the important thing is that the people, events, or companies mentioned regularly are usually highly regarded in the industry.

Further, it is generally assumed by the reader that "news" is generated by the publication—not by the company. In other words, the subject is reported on because the publication considers it important. (Product releases are generally sent *to* a publication, and most readers are at least sophisticated enough about the publishing field to know it.)

What we are leading up to is simply this: Getting written about in a publication's news section establishes a company or individual as a newsmaker of sorts. When the company or its executives are rarely mentioned, the reader takes little heed of the fact. But when the mentions come frequently and in different publications, the reader notices. It's then that the reader begins to regard the company or its executives as entities that *deserve* regular mentions—that is, because the company is a leader or its executives are authorities. It is substantially better for these mentions to appear in numerous publications. Appearing too frequently in just one magazine might arouse suspicions that the editor is a friend, that the company is an advertiser, or that some kind of nefarious deal might have been struck.

TALKING UP A STORM

Interestingly, getting these news mentions into a publication isn't really restricted to an exclusive circle of important companies or industry authorities. Of course, the established leaders and authorities tend to be favored. An editor would love to fill his columns with juicy morsels inspired by major companies or with quotes by nationally known authorities. But firms and executives with less stature stand an excellent chance of making it, too—particularly when the news has some creative touch or hits a "buzz" topic with an interesting point of view. That's part of the trick. The other part is to issue enough executive-statement news releases to break through the publication's "snob barrier." Editors who receive news regularly about a company eventually become familiar with it. They may even begin to follow news about the company and come to regard it, as readers do, as a leader in the field.

In one instance (not an isolated one by any means), a tiny, unknown company in the electronics industry pitted itself against some of the industry's giants. By issuing executive-statement news releases regularly, it wasn't long before it began appearing in the news columns of major industry publications. And it wasn't long, either, before editors began calling the company's top executives to interview them over the phone, seeking their comments about what was going on in the industry.

As with product releases, it is important to launch executive-statement releases as part of a *campaign*. It takes a steady stream of these releases before any decent sort of in-print batting average can develop. To increase opportunities for generating such releases, statements can come from the mouths of more than one company executive. For example, the president might talk about the future of the industry, the executive vice president might state something about sales, the marketing director might give his views on new market potentials, and the head of engineering might issue a statement on the company's realignment of engineering personnel responsibilities as a result of an important new order or development. Month after month, editors would receive a variety of newsy statements from the company. And they would probably be moved to use a few of them after they began getting acquainted with the company. Such a campaign has even been known to inspire editors, interested in topics of their own creation, to contact the executives (whom they have now begun to regard as authorities) and interview them for their opinions.

In brief, the executive-statement release is an effective means of getting into news sections and opens doors for a good deal of other editorial treatments, all of which can lead to a leadership image for the company and an authority image for its top-echelon employees.

What to Say

With a PR vehicle offering such great promise, it is worth delving into it a bit to see just what kinds of executive statements can be issued. That way, you too can target a stream of them at the media.

In many cases, company executives assume that the purpose of a press-release statement is merely to report some change or development of significance at a company. That's right, as far as it goes. But executive-statement news releases needn't be limited to important company developments. If they were, few releases could be generated about the average company because really newsworthy events are few and far between.

But if other than company matters are considered, then a whole new world of possibilities opens up. The secret of generating a steady flow of executive-statement releases is in not merely considering what is happening at the company. Consider, instead, what is happening out there in the world that can impinge on the company, its industry, its customers, its vendors, its shareholders, and its personnel. The possibilities are virtually endless. And when a company executive sounds off on them, it can make interesting reading. Usually, it scarcely matters whether the executive is for or against an issue. Either way, it's an opportunity to make news. In fact, a statement from an executive saying that he's not sure how something affects his company or the industry can also present such an opportunity. In one instance, the failure to take the "I-don't-know" approach caused a client to miss out on an important opportunity to make news. The client, which marketed regionally to companies within the state, was affected by a Justice Department decision that embraced its entire industry. Whether its prospective customers would gain or lose by the decision and whether it would encourage them to do business with the client was uncertain. Nevertheless, a fine opportunity existed to make some statement to the local media that were interested in the decision and its consequences. The PR consultant urged his client to follow immediately on the heels of the Justice Department announcement with an executive-statement release of its own on the meaning of the decision to local businessmen. Business editors of all the newspapers in the state would, in all likelihood, have welcomed—if not used—this information. And the client would have come off to the local business community as an authority that the media contacted for an expert opinion.

Unfortunately, the story does not have a happy ending. Unsure of the exact impact of the decision, the client contacted Washington for further clarification. Unable to obtain that, it opted not to issue the news release.

The important message here is that executive-statement opportunities should be sought out—whether or not all i's are dotted on facts relative to the issue in question. Also, when an opportunity presents itself, run, don't walk. Issue a statement immediately

—before a competitor has a chance to do so and before the issue becomes as stale as yesterday's news.

By issuing a timely release, a company can gain a great deal of favorable fallout. Besides getting into the media as written, the release might lead to after-the-fact followups by TV and radio news staffs seeking in-depth interviews. All of this goes a long way in helping establish that important leader/authority image.

Of course, opportunities like the Justice Department decision don't come along every day. What then can a company do to get news section exposure? A lot.

Using the executive-statement news release as the basic vehicle, a little creativity will launch a thousand press-release topics. To find the topics, you need to know what is going on in the industry. But that knowledge isn't limited to people who have been in the industry for years. A good PR firm should be able to apply its techniques to any client's situation in any number of industries.

The way to come by industry-related topics, whether you're totally immersed in the industry or not, is by perusing its trade publications. Free-lance writers who write authoritative articles often get their germinal ideas through the trade press. Back issues of publications in clients' fields have provided this writer with unending executive-statement topics over the years.

Probably the best way to approach the project is to clip all items that smack of possibilities, make a list of them, and present that list to company executives who are to be quoted in the releases. Then, with a tape recorder turned on, question an executive on one or more of the listed items. For some of the topics, he may agree with the point of view expressed in the clipped item; for others, he may not. And he may dismiss some of the topics as irrelevant. By the time the taping session is over, you should be armed with material for possibly a dozen or more executive-statement releases, including topics that came up on the spur of the moment during the taping. Reference to information provided in the original clippings will probably furnish additional material that can be used in writing the release, making the executive's statement sound even more knowledgeable.

Don't get the mistaken idea that finding topics by scanning trade magazines is easy. Take it from one who has done this for years and years: It takes hours and lots of magazines before a usable list materializes. You have to start with some idea of what kind of topic discussed by your company executive would interest an editor. That certain "feel"—call it creativity—comes from practice. Like anything else, it comes from having certain initial attempts rejected by editors and then adjusting your ideas accordingly. Experience, after all, is still the best teacher.

A list of the kinds of topics that can be used in executive-statement releases would be a good starting point. Those listed below are of two types: The kind you will find in a trade magazine and the kind that are based on internal company matters. Referring to this list, or one like it, will help you generate scads of executive-statement releases—on a continuous basis.

- Views on new legislation affecting the industry
- Views on raw material availability, or on pricing
- Views on manufacturer-distributor relationships
- Long and short term industry forecasts
- Company sales forecasts
- Views on new, just-over-the-horizon manufacturing techniques
- Views on the economy as it affects the industry or certain items in the line
- Comments on recent industry trade shows attended by the company
- Comments on new markets opening up or old ones drying up
- Comments on industry trends
- Comments on market research techniques and/or the industry's use of marketing information
- Comments on recent market research studies conducted by the company
- Comments on industry safety practices or environmental protection measures
- Announcements of new marketing programs launched by the company
- Views on export/import matters
- Views on foreign competition or on foreign market opportunities
- Announcements of company acquisitions
- Announcements of new company-to-company affiliations: Licensing agreements, contracts, etc.

- Announcements of executive-responsibility shifts
- Announcements of new equipment and its marketing significance
- Announcements of major new systems and their benefits to the customer
- New product announcements.

A Simple Twist

The last item, "new product announcements," may come as a surprise, since an entire chapter has already been devoted to product releases. Bear in mind, though, that product releases are limited to the product section of the publication. Imagine the increased attention the product would command if it were to appear in the highly read news section. How is this possible? It can be done simply by dressing the release in executive-statement trappings, so it reads like a news announcement from the mouth of an executive. There is an important difference in the way a strict product release and the executive-statement release are written. The former contains no quotes; has no attribution to a company executive, engineer, or scientist; and talks only about the product and, perhaps, its applications.

The executive-statement release, however, does not dwell on product alone. It may talk about the marketing significance of the new development, its importance to the company and its customers, and/or the changes it may bring about in the industry—all done as statements by an executive.

To see the difference more clearly, let's take a fictitious product and treat it both ways.

First, the product release.

FOR IMMEDIATE RELEASE   CONTACT: JOHN JONES
NEW XYZ WIDGET DESIGNED FOR LOW TEMPERATURE APPLICATIONS
ANYTOWN, USA, May 23—A new low-temperature widget has been developed by XYZ Company. The device, based on the evolving gizmo technology, is specifically designed to function in subzero temperatures. It will treble the longevity of equipment and devices dependent on electronics in arctic climates, outer space, and experi-

mental cryogenic vessels. XYZ is a major cryotechnology company known worldwide for its contributions to the electronics industry.

XYZ's latest widget, called "Cryotrone," is designed to operate in the 100-to-500-volt range. Only 1/8″ × 3/8″, it is ideal for printed circuit board installations. Its operating temperature range is −300°C to −25°C. Above that, electrical output becomes nonlinear.

XYZ's Cryotrone is currently available at a unit price of $35 in 1000-lot quantities. Delivery is 10 weeks. For additional information, contact Dept. Z, XYZ Company, P.O. Box 37, Anytown, USA.

Some product releases are longer, and some are shorter. The important point is that the release does not wander from product, application, price, availability, and how to obtain additional information. Such a release is tailored to meet the requirements of most publication product sections. In many instances, the product editor does little or no editing and runs the release virtually as is.

If, however, the release is written in a quotation format, an editor might have some difficulty running it. Being neither fish nor fowl—neither a straight product release nor appropriate for the publication's news section—it would in all likelihood end up in the round file, simply because other releases received by the editor offer less of a rewrite problem and are therefore easier to use.

However, there is a way to convert a release intended for the product section into one acceptable in the news section. It can be converted to an executive-statement release. Here's how it might appear.

FOR IMMEDIATE RELEASE   CONTACT: JOHN JONES
XYZ TO MAKE MAJOR BID FOR CRYO MARKET, SAYS SMITH

ANYTOWN, USA, May 23—In what represents its first major product introduction in three years, XYZ's just-developed Cryotrone will significantly increase the company's market share in outer space technology, according to company president John Smith.

"Cryotrone will triple the life of tomorrow's space vehicle," Smith pointed out. "That fact, alone, should save our government billions of dollars."

As a result of its recent product introduction, the company, Smith anticipates will have a "decided edge now over competition in the battle for sales in the subzero electronics market."

XYZ's president pointed out that the government is not the only sector to benefit from the development of Cryotrone. "It will allow XYZ to carve out an important position in arctic climate research technology and in the growing field of cryogenic vessels."

The new widget, currently completing tests in Antarctica, will be available, according to Smith, within ten weeks at the thousand-lot price of $35 per unit. Smith noted that the device, a product of the recent developments in gizmo technology, has been under development at XYZ's Georgia research facility for the past three years. "That's given us time to develop a worldwide distribution network." The company's sales and applications engineers, he said, will launch simultaneous presentations in Europe, the United Kingdom, and the United States beginning next week.

XYZ Company is a major factor in the cryotechnology field. It is known worldwide for its contributions to the electronics industry.

This release, obviously written for the news section of a publication, talks about marketing opportunities, share of market, and competitive edge, as well as product data. It manages to point out, too, that the company has an R&D facility in Georgia. The release was written as if a reporter had sought out XYZ's president to interview him on a development that is expected to dislocate current marketing positions enjoyed by other companies. It comes off as a significant piece of solid news. Most important, it provides a valuable means of getting product information out of the less-than-prestigious product section of a publication and into the more prestigious news section.

The techniques used here are easily transferable: Any product release can be converted to an executive-statement release. Since the two types of releases are directed at different editors, it is not a question of opting for one or the other. Both can be aimed at the same publication, simultaneously. One caution, however. As we've seen, there are lots of different executive-statement-release opportunities for getting into print. Overdoing the product type can start raising the news editor's eyebrow as to its credibility. It's best to use some judgment here, reserving the product-type executive-statement release for occasions when there is truly something legitimate to crow about. The first of an entire new line of products can certainly be expected to have some repercussions—however modest—in the marketplace. But issuing an executive-statement release for each addition to that product line would be a bit much.

4

The Feature Article

The old standby of company PR, the feature article, offers still another opportunity for exposure. Many people consider it to be the be-all and end-all of publicity. However, like the product release and the executive-statement release, the feature article is useful only in certain situations. In this chapter, we'll examine just where and when it is an appropriate public relations vehicle—that is, which PR strategies it best serves.

Getting Editors Interested

Before considering strategy, however, it is important to learn how to get a feature article into print. One way is to have the publication write it. But first it is necessary to provide an editor with the basic information he needs—just enough to attract his interest. This can be done effectively through either a backgrounder or a query letter.

THE BACKGROUNDER

Backgrounders are extremely useful PR vehicles. In the majority of cases, they are not written to be full-fledged articles in themselves. Rather, they are meant to supply information to an editor—much like an in-depth interview. An editor will then use the information by itself or combine it with information derived from other sources—interviews, literature searches, etc.—and shape it into a staff-written piece. The result may be an article devoted solely to the company's developments or a roundup that includes developments by other companies. An editor may even use bits and pieces of information from the backgrounder in a general article on the subject.

For an editor to use the backgrounder as a source for his own piece, it is probably best that it doesn't look like an article. If it does, an editor might suspect that competing publications are printing the very same material in the same words. Unlike articles, backgrounders are presented to the media on a nonexclusive basis, allowing anyone to draw material from them, even at the same time.

If not written like an article, how is a backgrounder written? There is no pat format. The backgrounder does what it must as simply as possible. Style is not important. Content is.

The best way to go about composing a backgrounder is to list all the bases that need to be covered. They may (or may not) include:

- A history of the company
- A history of the development of the product or service
- The background of all personnel involved in the development
- A history of the industry's problem prior to the product development
- An overview of development: What it is, told in a nontechnical way
- The requirements for producing the product; e.g., types of equipment, factory size, personnel skills, time, and special materials or techniques
- Problems, obstacles, limitations
- A detailed technical discussion of development (if a technical subject is involved)
- Charts
- Photos or drawings
- Sources for additional information
- A current user list

Each of these areas can become a backgrounder subject, with a paragraph or more covering the subject suggested by the subhead. It can be in outline form, with bulleted phrases; in full, paragraphed sentences; or a combination of the two. The number of pages depends on how long it takes to cover the essential areas.

More than ten pages would probably exhaust an editor and discourage him from reading on. But below that, length can vary all over the lot.

Backgrounders are normally handed out at media events or mailed to editors. They are generally part of a press kit and usually do not stand alone. Other press material is included in the kit, such as press releases, photos of the product, photos of product applications, and possibly photos of whoever is responsible for development of the product. If mailed to editors, a covering letter signed by a company executive or a PR professional is also included. Sometimes, a sample of the product—if small enough—can be enclosed in the kit. Catalogue sheets, brochures, or specification sheets may also be part of the kit, though they should not make an editor feel that the product or service has been on the market for a long time, destroying its news value. It would definitely be discouraging to an editor to find in the kit a reprint of a previously published article on the subject.

The backgrounder will give an editor an opportunity to staff-write the article if he chooses to. But all is not lost if he chooses not to. The press release, photos, and charts included in the kit will give him material he can just drop in if a hole exists in the news or product sections of his publication.

THE QUERY LETTER

Yet another means of soliciting editors is the telephone, but it is not particularly useful. Some PR people expect immediate go-aheads by just dialing a number. But few editorial acceptances are given on the spot. Usually, the editor asks for a written outline of the idea and makes a decision only after examining the outline. It is not uncommon for PR people to contact scores of editors from different publications, engage in time-consuming phone conversations, and come up with nothing.

A better choice is the query letter, an extremely effective art form used by free-lance writers, which can be sent simultaneously to a broad list of editors. Each of the letters should, of course, be individualized—that is, written to a specific editor or reporter by name. However, the contents of the letters can be identical. Persons with access to word-processing equipment can run off droves of such letters in virtually no time at all.

The advantage of the query letter is that it enables the PR professional to probe a large number of editors at the same time. Chances are, most of the responses will come back within a short time, allowing the PR practitioner to consider them as a whole and pick the most promising opportunities.

There is no need to grant exclusivity to a publication that plans to have the article staff-written. The article will be worded differently from one written by yourself or by any other publication. Should an editor ask the company to write it, then the article must be offered on an exclusive basis, with no other periodical receiving the identical (or near-identical) wording. There is one exception to this rule: The regional publication. Since they go to different regions of the country, such publications are not in conflict with each other. Because of that, the same article usually can be offered to several regional publications. In one instance, I placed an article on the use of industrial wiping cloths in 15 regional purchasing publications. In a few cases, the editor added the name of the local distributor at the end of the article, strictly for the convenience of his regional readers.

Should a query letter elicit a commitment from a truly appropriate publication before responses from other publications come in, it is worthwhile to jump at the opportunity. But if only a mediocre offer presents itself before you receive other responses, it is generally better to wait till the other responses arrive.

As mentioned previously, the query letter is an art form. However, since the subject is adequately covered in readily available books and articles, there is no point in going into detail here. Suffice it to say that the letter should not be long and drawn out, nor should the main attraction be buried in the second or later paragraphs. Instead, the letter should be written with the most compelling, earth-shattering, or enticing bit of information about the subject in the first sentence—so it's the first thing to strike the editor's eye. A couple of paragraphs will do—all containing action-packed sentences aimed at grabbing and holding the editor's interest. The query letter can also be used to stimulate interest in an interview.

TO AUTHOR OR NOT TO AUTHOR

Once one or more publications have agreed to run a feature article about your company, you must decide (in consultation with each publication) who will write it—or, more properly, who will appear to have written it—the company or the publication.

It cannot be emphasized too strongly that an article by-lined by someone from the company, one that is by-lined by someone from the publication, and one that is not by-lined at all are strategically different vehicles. For example, a feature article obviously written by a company representative would seem like an outright plug for the company. The same article written by a member of the publication staff would be far more effective. And even a non-by-lined version—whether written by someone from the company or by someone from the publication—would be better because the reader has no way of determining who wrote the article.

Both publication-by-lined and non-by-lined articles carry with them third-party endorsements. Evidently—the reader assumes—if the publication is devoting editorial space to a product, it must think highly of the product. But if the publication wrote (or appears to have written) the article, it must think *very* highly of the product. In short, an article actually or apparently written by the publication has far greater credibility than an article written by the company. And, with PR, credibility is the name of the game.

Understanding the Types

Now let's consider four frequently used types of feature articles: The case history, the state-of-art, the roundup, and the how-to. Each of them, we'll discover, has a different PR function and satisfies a different company need. Thus, it is not enough to place any feature article with any publication. It is important to single out precisely what strategy is called for and to prepare an article relating to that strategy.

The case history describes the experience that a person, company, or institution has had with a product, service, system, or procedure. The objective of this kind of article is to tell the reader that the experience has been positive—that the product, for example, does what it's supposed to do. In most instances, the article begins by stating that the user is satisfied with the product. Then it describes the problem the user had before buying the product. Finally, it shows how the product solved the problem. Sometimes, case histories, written as third-person reports, are devoid of direct quotations expressing the user's satisfaction. However, some publications prefer a less formal approach and opt for articles written in the first person and sprinkled liberally with quotes.

The state-of-the-art article discusses a product or system in its most recent stage of development. From the point of view of the reader, its objective is tutorial—to explain the latest technological advance in a particular product category or technical area. From the PR practitioner's point of view, this type of article is usually aimed at convincing the reader that the latest design of one brand makes it more effective or less expensive than other brands with a similar function. Such an article frequently starts out by describing the shortcomings of the existing technology and then discusses the benefits offered by the most recent advance. Once the reader's appetite is whetted, the article turns technical. At this point, the more complicated aspects of the new development are unwrapped, the degree of detail varying with the type of publication the article will appear in. Should the difficult matter be introduced at the beginning, the reader might never get beyond the first sentence. As with all article writing, the most interesting, attention-getting, least-difficult-to-grasp information should be up front for the reader to see first, followed by the drier, less appealing material.

The roundup article is exactly what its name implies: A roundup of information related to a particular subject. The subject can be a product category or a type of service. In some instances, the article is written without quotations, in which case the author is solely responsible for its contents. Another type of roundup is full of quotes from authorities in a field related to the subject under discussion. The latter is usually drafted by a magazine's editorial staff. The former is generally authored by someone from a company. Often, products or services from different companies are compared, and those generated by the company that writes the article are shown to be superior to those of other companies. Products or services can be described in great detail. The author can begin with a particular point of view (e.g., transistors are better than vacuum tubes) and then support his premise with examples taken from the various available products or services.

The how-to article explains to the reader how to do something —buy a bathing suit, build a house, shop for life insurance, or select a particular type of electronic component. The article normally explains the need for the product or service in question and then makes a case for the difficulties involved in making the right selection or taking the proper approach. The article then describes in detail the issues that should be considered, illustrating them with numerous examples. When a magazine staffer produces the article, it usually deals with the various alternatives in a fair, even-handed way. But the PR-initiated article stacks the deck in favor of the company's product or service. This is generally accomplished by establishing criteria that favor the company's offering.

Choosing the Right Type

Like the product release, the feature article can publicize the product or service. And like the executive-statement release, it can improve the company's image and enhance the reputation of its executives. In each case, however, some kinds of feature articles work better than others.

What PR objectives can be achieved by the case-history article? Obviously, since it deals with the use of a product by a company or consumer, it will reflect well on the manufacturer—at least, as far as the product is concerned. As we've seen, however, product is not the buyer's only consideration in making a purchase. What if the case history deals with speed of installation or delivery and the savings in time or dollars for the product's end-user? Then the article positions the manufacturer in a good light in terms of these considerations. However, it doesn't position the company as having good vendor relations, being financially stable, leading the industry in technological development, or anything else. The case-history article emphasizes only those aspects of the company that pertain to one customer's use of its product or service. And those aspects may not be enough to make for a successful sale.

Now consider the state-of-art article. There are, in general, two tacks it can take. It can describe a company's latest technological innovation. Or it can provide an overview of recent technological developments in an industry. The latter is really a specific form of roundup article.

Two different PR objectives can be achieved with the state-of-art article. First, a company can be positioned as a pioneer in a certain technology or discipline. Second, a company executive, scientist, or engineer can be established as an authority in the field. The first objective is best accomplished by an article that either carries no by-line or is by-lined by someone at the publication. If the breakthrough is both original and important, the announcement of it will gain a measure of credibility if a third-party —a magazine staff writer—writes the article, with or without a by-line. The second objective can be achieved if a company spokesman writes the article and uses his by-line. While the company-by-lined article may not establish the company as a leader in the field, it can elevate the stature of the author in the eyes of the company's various publics. He shows himself to be knowledgeable about the industry, aware of its technology, and therefore an expert on the subject. Furthermore, the fact that he might have been asked by the publication to write the article at least implies that his expertise is recognized by others.

On the other hand, as beneficial as it might be for company prestige, the company-written, *non-by-lined* state-of-art article is not too popular among editors. This is because a non-by-lined article leads the reader to believe that the publication's staff wrote it. If the article turns out to be misleading or deceptive, the publication would be to blame in the eyes of its readers and advertisers. The responsibility for the reliability of a *company*-by-lined state-of-art article, however, rests with the company and the employee who wrote it—not the publication. For that reason, editors are more apt to accept it.

However, editors don't always reject company-written, non-by-lined articles. And because there is much to gain if such an article is accepted, the gamble is worth taking. Furthermore, if the attempt fails, it will still be possible to get the article published without a company by-line—that is, by getting the magazine interested in having one of its own staff do the article, probably by interviewing one or more of the company's people. Then, when the article appears, since it will carry the by-line of one of the publication's staff, editorial endorsement will be implied.

What about the by-line question as it pertains to the roundup article? If such an article is written on a particular subject by someone from a company, the article will, most probably, carry that author's by-line. The magazine will not risk omitting it, for reasons we've already examined. However, a roundup article that carries a publication-staff by-line or no by-line at all (implying it was staff-written) has the credibility of a third-party endorsement.

Do the same arguments for and against by-lines pertain to the how-to article? This kind of feature article is a popular vehicle among PR practitioners. However, it does little to position a company as a leader. It is more apt to position the author, whose by-line it carries, as an authority.

As the preceding discussion shows, feature articles are not everything they are frequently thought to be. The case-history feature can gain acceptance for a product or some other aspect of a company's operation—particularly if the article appears to be written by the publication. But it does little for the *overall* image of the company. The state-of-art article, if it appears to have been written by the publication, *can* lend prestige to a company. When it is by-lined by someone from the company, however, its strategic value is to position the author as an authority. As we'll see later, there are certain strategies that demand such an approach. Written by an outside source, the roundup article is hard to get accepted without a company by-line. With a by-line, it helps establish the author as an authority. The how-to is another example of an article that does little for the prestige of a company. But it does show off the author as an authority and, as such, adds some indirect prestige to his company. The how-to article that is written by a publication's staff—if it dwells on a company's product or service—can generate acceptance for that product or service, but it contributes little to the general reputation of the company.

As we've seen, what determines the strategic value of a feature article is not only what kind of feature it is, but who wrote it (or appears to have written it)—someone from the company or someone from the publication. That often-overlooked element has a powerful influence on how the article is received by readers.

Getting the Article Read

In articles intended to entertain, the opening paragraphs can be witty, philosophical, mysterious, conversational, historical, or anecdotal. They are meant to be amusing, intriguing, or distracting. The PR article, too, targeted at a trade or industrial publication, can use any of these stylistic ploys. Whatever its approach, however, the article must be written with the understanding that the reader is coming to it for entirely different reasons—that he is not reading the article as a pleasant way to pass the time. Instead, trade or industrial magazines are read because they help the reader do better in his business or profession. That might include increasing sales, improving efficiency, or developing new technologies. The reader reads the article for what he can get out of it to benefit him in his business or professional life.

For that reason, such an article must grab the reader immediately and tell him right off that he will benefit by reading it. That point is best made in the first few words or sentences. As a business magazine reader, I am too busy to spend time on an article that does not offer that promise. Finding out that it does after the first few sentences is finding out too late. Either I know right away that there's something in the trade magazine article for me or I move on to the next one.

How does an article hold the business reader for even a few seconds? By jamming every important point in the article into the first sentence. Normally, long and complicated sentences are frowned on in all areas of business writing. Short, pithy ones are preferred. However, a business-type reader is usually willing to read one sentence. And if that sentence fails to interest him, he'll turn the page or find something else to do.

But attracting the reader in the space of one sentence is not easy. If all the important information in the article can be summarized in five words, good. If not, the sentence ought to go on and on until all the essentials are covered. That might be thirty words. In fact, the entire first paragraph might be one sentence.

Of course, all the fine points of style learned in writing courses will help. But my own experience (as a reader and PR practitioner) tells me that nothing can take the place of saying enough in the first sentence to make the reader want to continue. Not that every benefit mentioned in the article must be stated there. But enough must be included to entice the reader to go on. The remaining opening remarks—whether in one, two, or more paragraphs—can be devoted to the rest of the benefits. But the grabber has to be right up front where the reader is sure to see it, where he's willing to devote a second or two to finding out if there's anything in it for him before wasting any more time. Flip through a number of articles in leading business magazines and you'll be amazed at how many of them make use of the long, all-encompassing first sentence.

Like the closing paragraphs of the written PR plan, the final words of an article are especially important. A reader who may have worked his way through several interruptions to the end of the article may have forgotten important details. Also, he may have skimmed, hoping that everything would come together by the time he reached the final paragraph. But if the article ends abruptly, with the final paragraph failing to reiterate major points, he'll probably not take the time to reread it. Then the value of the article as a PR piece—intended to lead the reader to some sort of action or conclusion—will have been lost.

Most experienced free-lancers who write for magazines will tell you that an article must have a good opening and a good close. That's because an editor generally looks at those portions of the article first when assessing the manuscript for his publication. Lacking either, the piece is apt to be rejected.

Thus, a PR article for a trade or industrial publication ought to end with a brief review of the benefits to the reader that were covered previously. This can be done in a single closing paragraph. And it can be done cleverly, using whatever sophisticated techniques the writer has at his command. But it must be done—for fear of losing the editor or reader.

Keeping the Article Working

One final item before closing our discussion of feature articles. Considering how valuable publicity exposure is, it would be a pity for it to die on the vine after the article's (or news item's) one-time appearance in a particular issue of a publication. But it needn't. There is a vehicle that can extend its life, possibly for years: The reprint. It can provide extra mileage for the article as salesperson-leave-behinds, mailers (often accompanied by a sales letter), clip-ons to proposals, and trade-show literature. In this form, the article-turned-reprint serves as support for whatever sales pitch is being given at the time, orally or in writing. In fact, the reprint becomes a prestige-builder in its own right, conveying to the prospect that the editor considered the company and its product or service so important he used valuable space in his publication for a writeup about it. The salesperson (or letter clipped onto the reprint, as in a mailing) can even establish that link by coming right out and saying it.

Even with article reprints, there are several strategic aspects to consider. Some PR practitioners believe that the most effective format for a reprint is not as an overt company promotion piece. Instead, the reprint should appear as if the publication ran off extra copies of an important article for the benefit of its readers. Done in that manner, the reprint might have a brochure format, with the cover of the magazine reproduced as its cover. A panel or inset on the cover might spotlight the title of the PR article or news item, as if it were truly a cover story.

Other PR people consider the reprint a wasted effort if it doesn't reflect that it is from the company discussed in the article. In that case, the name, logo, and address of the company would appear on it. In some instances, an ad for the product or service mentioned might even be printed on the back page.

However, the first approach is strategically more appealing. The more the reprint appears as if the publication intended it for its readers, the greater its credibility and the more prestige it lends to the company.

The second approach, which is used more frequently, smacks of propaganda and, therefore, I'm convinced, provides less credibility. To get the best of both worlds, merely clip a salesperson's business card to the first type of reprint. It then appears that the company obtained reprints that the publication ran off for its own readers. That's putting a little more finesse into the business of reprints. And a lot more credibility.

5

Prestige-Building Situations

Despite the attempt to plan for every conceivable public relations opportunity, the PR program cannot account for everything. Not all situations can be foreseen, and not all contingencies can be planned for. Nevertheless, the unexpected will inevitably occur. And the PR practitioner must be ready for it when it does.

Interviews

One category of the unexpected can be easily prepared for: Media responses to official company announcements. Whether the company news is disseminated through a product release or a press briefing, editors may want to know more. Unprepared for, the request for additional information may result in a variety of problems—a show of ignorance on the part of an unbriefed chief executive, the release of sensitive information by an overeager engineer, or a refusal to comment from a diffident marketing director. Prepared for, however, these problems can be avoided. In fact, requests for supplementary information can be transformed into additional PR opportunities.

One such opportunity is the interview—either about a new product mentioned in a product release or about any of the executive-statement topics cited in Chapter 3. Aware that any public communication can result in a phone call from or an impromptu visit by an editor or reporter, many PR practitioners try to prepare the potential subject of the interview for such a possibility.

To enable the executive to handle the interview successfully, the PR person must do his homework, which entails a careful analysis of the contents of the release or briefing. First, he should determine what additional information the interviewer might want or need. Second, he should pick out "sensitive areas" (if there are any) and formulate plausible responses to possible questions about them. For example, if a new product has been under development for three years, an editor might ask if the technological know-how required to develop the product coincided with what might be construed as a "raid" three years previously on a competitor's scientific staff, resulting in the hiring of five of its top people. Although such questions are loaded, they cannot be dismissed. They require candid and deft responses.

This doesn't mean that executives should shy away from releasing statements to the media in order to avoid in-depth probing or misinterpretation. Quite the contrary. This "ripple" effect can lead to some highly valuable editorial exposure. But it is worth doing a little extra homework to make certain all interview questions can be accurately and strategically answered.

Of course, this may mean going beyond the executive who was quoted in the release. Finding answers to all the potential questions raised by the release might require visits to several executives, scientists, or engineers within the company to hear how they would respond. Then, with the help of the executive to be interviewed—and possibly others—the best answer to each question can be settled on.

If possible, the PR person should ask the editor to submit an advance list of questions that will be asked during the interview. Some editors welcome such requests, hoping that the answers will be better researched and will represent the official views of the company, rather than the opinions of one executive.

But editors do not always provide advance notification of an interview. After receiving the release, they may just call the executive and try to get unrehearsed responses. That is why it's good practice for the PR practitioner to do all the backup research on potential questions and sensitivities *before* the release goes out. Then the executive will have been primed ahead of time for that "unexpected" phone call, eliminating the possibility of awkward and embarrassing answers to an editor's probing.

The same problem can arise at press conferences and briefings. The company that believes the invited media representatives will "stick to the script" is putting its head in the sand. And such probing is not limited to U.S. editors. In the U.K. and elsewhere in Europe, editors at press conferences typically delve into matters outside the subject area of the conference or briefing—such as rumor that an executive is leaving the company or a news item suggesting that a corporate takeover is in the works.

When any news is announced at a media event, reporters and editors should be expected to come up with embarrassing questions of this sort. They may relate to alleged weaknesses in technology or a reported supply shortage in the industry. Or they may touch on previous failures in marketing or new product development. The possibilities for embarrassment are endless.

However, trying to figure out in advance just what questions might be raised is far from easy. If a company has been having financial difficulties, it would be smart to include at the event a knowledgeable company executive representing that sector of the business—just in case. Should someone then raise a touchy financial issue, that executive would be the one to handle it.

Exposure to sensitive questions gains more significance as the level of the executive to be interviewed increases. If the president or board chairman is scheduled for an interview, the PR professional had better do all he can to brief him fully on all the potential questions and rehearse with him the best answers. Too often it is assumed that lower-level executives are not aware of all the issues while the chief executive is. That is definitely not the case. The lofty position of the latter doesn't necessarily make him aware of everything or enable him to field touchy questions in the best way. But a wrong answer coming from him can create tidal waves instead of ripples.

In one instance, the newly-appointed president of a major company turned out to be an excellent vehicle for getting news of the company into the media. He was well spoken, handled himself confidently under fire, and was newsworthy because he had just replaced the previous president. However, being new to that position, he was not all that well informed about everything going on in the company. Without intense rehearsals prior to editor interviews (of which there were many), he might—innocently enough —have given misleading information or provided strategic insights to competitors.

Roundups

Another PR opportunity not directly under the control of the PR practitioner or company executive—for contents, timing, or topic —is the roundup article. Yet, it is perhaps one of the most powerful vehicles for positioning a company as a leader and its executives as industry authorities.

The roundup is usually inspired by the editorial staff of a publication. Oddly enough, however, in spite of image-building potential, the roundup is often overlooked as a PR vehicle.

This kind of feature article discusses a subject generally related to an industry or to a practice within that industry. It covers the subject broadly—possibly its history, its present and future status, and the major companies and personalities involved with the subject in some way, as manufacturers, end-users, or middlemen. The PR value of the roundup stems from the editor's need to support statements he makes in the article. He does this by quoting leading executives in the industry or experts on the subject of the article and by discussing what major firms are contemplating, planning, or doing.

The key words here are *leading* executives and *major* firms. Readers of a roundup article are quick to pick up on the names of companies and individuals cited, regarding them from that point on as firms and people of some repute in the field. (Why else would an editor quote or refer to them to support his article?) And this is precisely why it is advantageous to be quoted or referred to in a roundup. Of course, such an article doesn't simply mention one person or company to support what its writer says. Usually, numerous ones are mentioned. And that's why being included among them is important. The reader is led to believe that all the companies or executives mentioned are equally significant in the field.

Some companies are dissuaded from suggesting a roundup idea to an editor or participating in a roundup article because no single company is highlighted. Many of my own clients originally felt that not standing alone but being named along with others diluted the publicity value.

However, by participating in a roundup article, a company is really obtaining a stage for its actors to play their parts on. Without that stage, the opportunity to be mentioned alongside industry leaders and for showing off the company capabilities simply wouldn't exist. Nevertheless, many executives persist in jealously hoping for the writeup that will mention them alone, little realizing that it is the association with the leading names in the industry that establishes the leadership/authority position they seek.

Meanwhile, how does one go about getting into roundups? Good things don't come easy. In this case, much of the work is time-consuming, rather than difficult. It involves finding out far in advance which publications are planning roundup articles on topics related to your industry or technology. And that's where the work come in. As with a press release, the search usually starts with the development of a media list. Often it can be the same list used in the press release program. These are the media whose audiences are potentially interested in your product, service, or company—be they buyers, vendors, financial analysts, private investors, or shareholders.

Once the media list is drawn up—conceivably hundreds of publications taken from several media directories—the real labor begins: Getting in touch with the editors, which can take the form of phone calls or letters. In my own experience, phone calls are generally more productive and more timely. Unless you know a specific department editor at a publication, it's usually best to start with the managing editor or editor-in-chief. They have first-hand knowledge of which articles are being prepared for future issues and, if one is in the works in your area of interest, can direct you to the editor or writer responsible for it.

At that point, a brief exchange of information takes place. The editor relates what, specifically, he is working on, and the PR professional suggests that one or more executives from his company can provide insights, opinions, or statistical information that can be plugged into the article. Often an editor will be overjoyed to receive this kind of help and will reel off a list of questions or topics that he'd like the company executive to respond to. The PR practitioner then reviews this with company people, determining the best responses to the questions and deciding which executive should be referred to as the source. The best way to convey the response to the editor is in writing. Tables, charts, drawings, or photos can be sent along, as well, if they help illustrate the executive's remarks.

Of course, there is no guarantee that the editor will use the material. However, there is a good chance he will—particularly if you've taken pains to have his questions answered accurately and fully. Furthermore, if an editor has received this kind of help from you on numerous occasions, he might begin to count on the executives of your company for authoritative information whenever he's writing on a subject in their area of expertise.

With regular appearances in such staff-written roundups—and multiplied over a wide range of publications—the company and its executives take on a new stature among readers of these publications. As a result of steady and broad exposure, they leap, in the readers' minds, from unknown or little-known entities to industry leaders and authorities. Reprints of such articles, with the quotes and company references circled in red, become excellent leave-behinds for salespeople, as well as clip-ons to letters mailed to prospects. Here, the object is to make the publicity exposure continue working for the company—long after it has appeared in the publication. Practiced assiduously, participation in roundups can have a powerful influence on the esteem in which your company and its executives are held.

Seminars

Another opportunity not usually initiated by or under the control of PR or company people—yet extremely prestige-building for executive and company alike—is the seminar. Scarcely an industry exists that doesn't sponsor such forums periodically. Some industries hold them once a year, while others have seminars throughout the year in different sections of the country or abroad.

Some seminars allow participants to have solo speaking roles. Those selected for such roles are normally recognized as authorities in the field. Other seminars have an audience/panel format in which participants speak briefly to specific issues or answer specific questions. While the latter type of seminar doesn't usually showcase individual speakers, panelists are nevertheless regarded with esteem by the attending audience.

Getting invited to participate at a seminar, however, doesn't necessarily require that a company be well known or well established. And that is why seminar participation is so beneficial in waging the leader/authority-image battle. Virtually anyone from any company in any industry can become a seminar participant. Like news releases, every bid for such exposure isn't necessarily successful. But constant striving can produce a decent batting average—not all hits, but not all misses, either.

Perseverance, then, is one of the important factors in securing participating roles in seminars. Another is being aware of the opportunities for participation. There are two types of seminars to be on the lookout for: One involves the company's own industry (including trade shows); the other involves industries to which the company markets its products or services. Information about both types can usually be found in trade publication listings of upcoming events in their own vertical industries. If such a listing is hard to come by, the industry trade association can usually supply it without too much difficulty.

At the first type of seminar—within the company's own industry—the participating speaker or panelist will, for the most part, be addressing his peers. Of course, they will be interested in the latest news and views relating to their own interests. At the second type, the participant will be addressing potential customers (or others he would like to influence). For example, a manufacturer of computers might have a product manager participate in a seminar for motel/hotel executives. His role could be to show them how to use and/or choose computers for their line of work. By addressing these executives, the product manager elicits their esteem and indirectly promotes his company's products, something his company's salespeople can cash in on at a later date. He or his salespeople may even have a one-on-one opportunity at the seminar to pursue the subject of discussion further with interested members of the audience—potential customers.

Contacting those who are responsible for arranging and running seminars is the next step in trying to become a participant. It might take several phone calls to zero in on the right party. When the right person is finally reached, he'll undoubtedly want to know specifically what contribution the company executive can make. Either what aspect of the seminar topic he could treat in depth, as a speechmaker; or what new angles, ideas, or approaches he could address as a panelist. Since all can be lost at that crucial moment (if the contact is made in person or by phone), it is important to have already chosen one or more "buzz" topics that will be of particular interest to the seminar audience. If the seminar arranger finds the topics relevant and the executive knowledgeable, he might accept the offer immediately. If he is uncertain, he may ask the executive to outline the topics in a letter.

Of course, whatever the topic discussed or ideas presented at the seminar, the participant should not directly promote his company or its products. It is far more credible to speak generically about the subject, without pushing the company's vested interest by brand name or specific model. That the participant is from a particular company should be enough to tell the audience indirectly—yet unmistakably—that the company's products or services can solve the problems or perform the tasks or satisfy the needs referred to in the executive's comments.

Of course, it is not always easy to convince company representatives, especially chief executives—to avoid self-promotion. The problem came up with one of my clients, who planned to participate in a national grocery industry seminar. So convinced was the company president of the widespread interest in his product that he resisted all attempts at dissuading him from an out-and-out dissertation on his product's benefits. The struggle lasted right up to the day before he left for the convention. Only then were the PR people and other company executives able to convince him that a generic treatment of the subject—without any mention of the brand—had far greater credibility and would cast him in the role of authority instead of huckster.

For regional seminars located far from corporate headquarters, company people in that region might be suggested as participants. For major events, however, executives from the home office might do well to travel out to the seminar. In one instance, a seminar held in California was considered so important to a company headquartered in England that it flew one of its executives across the Atlantic to participate. The seminar was conducted by a publication in the company's field, which published a full report on the seminar, with extensive quotes by the client. There was no question that the client and its executives were regarded by readers of the report as significant entities in the industry. And the cost of the trip was amply compensated by this substantial enhancement of the company's reputation.

Making More of a Good Thing

Although arranging for seminar participation can be time-consuming, it can be extremely worthwhile. This is so because the benefits of participation are not exhausted at the seminar itself. In fact, the initial, relatively small-scale exposure can be turned in to a reusable asset that reaches a large and valuable audience. This can be done in several ways. First, after a company representative has been invited to participate as a speaker or panelist, a news release should be issued stating that fact and directed at all appropriate media—particularly those targeted at the relevant industry or industries.

Then, as soon as the seminar is over, a news release should be issued giving the name and position of the participant and summarizing his contribution. That release might be accompanied by a head-and-shoulders photo of the participant or one that shows him in his seminar role, either addressing the audience or at the panelist table.

Arrangements can also be made in advance with reporters or editors attending the seminar to interview the company's participant before or after the seminar. Letting media people in on the topic ahead of time can result in some beneficial exposure—particularly if time and place are arranged at the seminar site where an exclusive, private interview can be conducted. It's even worthwhile, for speaking-role participation, to make copies of the talk and a photo of the speaker available to members of the press at the seminar.

Photos are important for several reasons. They can mean the difference between a brief mention in a publication and more extensive coverage. In many cases, the news item mentioning a company and/or its executive may be simply a listing, with similar mention of other companies and their people. But an accompanying photo can make the executive and his company appear to be more important than participants whose photos were not run. It's a simple device, but it can add immeasurably to the company's leader/authority image.

One example will suffice. A number of advertising agencies recently won prestigious awards for their creative work. When the media followed this up with a story about the awards, all agencies but one were merely mentioned in a long string of agency names. Because it had provided the media with a photo of its principals, that agency stood out over all the others because the media used its photo. It was the only agency that received more than a one-liner, making it more important to the reader than the other agencies.

A company's participation in a seminar can also provide the basis for a string of executive-statement news releases. The major points raised in the talk can become stand-alone topics about which individual releases can be written.

If a participating company's potential customers are located near the seminar site, they can be invited to the seminar by the company. Besides image-building, this gives salespeople an opportunity to meet prospects without having to set up a formal appointment.

If the seminar is part of a trade show at which the participant's company is an exhibitor and at which a trade show daily is distributed, the company can promote its seminar participation in that medium. Usually, trade show dailies are the work of an industry periodical trying to gain status and additional exposure for itself among potential advertisers and subscribers. The editors of the daily are generally eager for whatever news can be generated during the show. A release about the seminar talk or an interview with the company speaker would probably be appreciated. As with other writeups, this too can be reprinted and distributed, so that it lives long after the show.

Naturally, the company spokesman at the seminar should speak and act as professionally as possible. That means the contents and delivery of his talk should be well prepared, preferably with the help of PR pros, who can offer sound advice and save a considerable amount of time. In particular, the use of graphics should be given serious consideration. There are few talks that can't be made more interesting by slides, charts, or easeled cue cards to highlight important points or phrases. While the company executive may have little time to prepare or little know-how in visual aids, these skills ought to be part of a PR person's bag of tricks. It is important, of course, to find out from the seminar arrangers what type of graphics will be allowed and what type of slide projectors, screens, overhead projectors, and chalk boards will be available. Nothing is worse than arriving with carefully prepared material for use with an overhead projector and finding that the only equipment on hand is for 35mm slides. Again, it is the responsibility of the PR staff to determine what equipment is allowable and available.

6

Dealing with the
Media

Some critics of public relations have argued that using the media to gain exposure, especially without paying for it, is manipulative —and even deceptive. After all, press releases, feature articles, and seminar speeches are self-promotional. Yet, the information presented through these PR vehicles is offered as "news." In this respect, the argument goes, the media are manipulated and the public is deceived.

However, this accusation is invalid on two grounds. First, the public wants and needs information about new products, new technologies, and new techniques in research, production, and marketing. Manufacturers are the major source of information in these areas. And, therefore, the media are forced to use them to satisfy their readers' needs. In fact, publishers and editors compete— often aggressively—for useful, interesting, and entertaining material. Presumably, when they find it, they print it. And the decision to print it is not based on whether it serves the interests of the company but whether it serves the interests of the media and the public.

Second, the self-serving nature of all public relations activities does not distinguish PR from other, seemingly less questionable, sources of information. When veterans march on Washington or governors hold press conferences, for example, they do so expressly to gain media exposure. However, the press may cover these events—if they are newsworthy. And the same criterion works for PR events, which, though similarly self-serving, may also be of interest to the public.

A public relations activity may be said to be manipulative when the information it conveys is false or misleading. And the point applies equally to the activities of interest groups and public officials. In all these cases, the media can be manipulated. Within the limits of time and budget, editors try to determine the reliability of their sources, the accuracy of their facts, and the news value of their information. But they don't always succeed. Sooner or later, an exaggeration, a distortion, or an outright misrepresentation gets through and the medium responsible must endure the inevitable loss of face—if not loss of advertising and readership.

However, the medium will not be the only victim. A company that tries to manipulate the media eventually gets caught. Then it might be a long time before its PR people get another story placed. The best bet in the long run (and companies are in business for the long run) is to be honest with the media, letting editors judge on the basis of the facts whether the material is too good to resist or deserves no media coverage.

Inspiring Confidence

The straightforward approach, practiced on a continuing basis, has the long-term benefit to the company (and PR practitioner) of fostering editor confidence. And that has a bearing of no little significance on whether material furnished to the editor will be published or not. In fact there are a number of ways of inspiring such confidence, most of which pertain to the content of the news release.

First, it is important to decide whose stationery the release should be printed on—the company's or the PR firm's. As a rule, it is better for a large or well-known company to use its own stationery. Editors will probably recognize the name and derive some measure of confidence from it, making the contents of the release more credible to them.

An unknown company stands a better chance of getting its press release published if it is printed on the stationery of a reliable public relations company or PR department of an advertising agency. It goes without saying that a PR firm stands to lose much more than its client does for misleading editors. And because editors realize that fact, they rely more on the information they receive from PR people. Should the source prove unreliable, the editor's welcome mat would be withdrawn—and the PR firm's releases would no longer be accepted by the publication.

Editors will also have more confidence in a release if they can contact someone directly for verification and additional information. The name and phone number of that person should appear at the top of the first page of the release, following the word "contact." Without it, an editor can waste precious time having his call transferred from person to person before reaching anyone who is knowledgeable about the release or authorized to speak about it. It's not unheard of for an editor, unable to reach the right company spokesperson, to turn to others in the field, even competitors, and get the information from them—sometimes to the detriment of the company that sent the release.

In fact, editors can be doggedly persistent in pursuit of information, and they will go to any source to get it. For this reason, it is important for the company contact to cooperate fully with the media whenever possible. In one instance, the editor of a major financial publication contacted a publicly owned instrument manufacturer for certain corporate information. The company's president instructed everyone to respond with "No comment" should he be contacted by that editor.

"No comment" it was. But that did not stop the editor. When the story finally broke into print, it was anything but flattering—probably because the company's competitors turned out to be the only sources available for information.

"No comment" ought to be *verboten* as a response to questions by the press. Of course, the information source should not be just anyone at the company. One person should be so designated, and all media people should be referred to him. This procedure eliminates the possibility of contradictory statements, which are sometimes overplayed by the media, to the chagrin of the company involved. For a company with plants scattered throughout the company, one person at each plant might be designated as the news source when local media come calling. But he must get the "party line" from the main information source at corporate headquarters.

If the company is a subsidiary or division of a fairly well-known organization, that relationship should be mentioned in the opening paragraph of the release. The sooner the parent company's name appears, the less likely will the release be committed to the round file. The same applies if the company is publicly owned. Of course, editors know that, in spite of their legal and moral responsibilities, public companies might still mislead the media. But because they are subject to the scrutiny of their shareholders, as well as the SEC, most editors feel they are less likely to take chances. The relevant information should be inserted in parentheses after the company name in the first paragraph: "listed, NYSE" or "listed, AMEX."

One of the simplest means of gaining an editor's respect is merely a one-paragraph appendage to the press release: The corporate paragraph. Although it rarely finds its way into print—because it is too strong a plug—it tells the editor who the company is and what it does. It reiterates the company's affiliation with a larger organization, lists its products or services, and identifies its major markets. Naturally, because the corporate paragraph should not interfere with the message embodied in the release, it should be placed at the very end—as the final paragraph.

Of course, appending a corporate paragraph to a release is only a beginning. The real value of identifying the company in this way comes from sending releases out on a regular basis. Faced with a release from a firm he doesn't know—even if it is identified in the corporate paragraph—the editor is forced to guess whether he should trust its contents and risk misleading his readers. After receiving several releases from the same source, however, he begins to feel less tentative about using its material. Seeing the same corporate paragraph in release after release, he gets to know the company and gains confidence in its communications.

Aiming the Release

Once you have positioned the release in a manner most likely to encourage editor confidence, you must decide which editors to send it to. Because of the relatively low cost of running off extra releases and the few extra cents worth of postage needed, releases ought to be distributed to the broadest possible audience—whoever might conceivably have some interest in the message. For that reason, besides a company's primary markets, secondary (and possibly tertiary) markets ought to be included on the publicity media list (provided the company has a sales force capable of covering the additional markets). That means using both horizontal and vertical media. Horizontal publications expose audiences in all markets to the company message. Vertical media reach other publics with which the company does business—suppliers and distributors and potential or existing customers in a specific field.

A word about developing comprehensive media lists. Although it is time-consuming, it is far from difficult. The most fertile sources are the various media directories. *Standard Rate & Data Service (SRDS),* available at most ad agencies, is really an entire family of directories, each listing a different type of medium: Radio, TV, business publications, consumer magazines, newspapers, etc. Most of the information contained in *SRDS* is categorized for easy reference. In the business publication directory, for example, magazines are grouped by industry. In the radio, TV, and newspaper directories, they are categorized by state and city. And in the consumer magazine *SRDS,* they are listed according to publication type (e.g., women's, men's, fashion). *SRDS* usually gives considerably more information than the PR practitioner needs. In addition to names and addresses of publications, it lists advertising reps, breaks down circulation, and provides such information as advertising rates, mechanical requirements for ads, closing dates, and special issues. It lists only media that accept advertising.

Bacon's Publicity Checker (which now comes in magazine and newspaper editions) is another directory that is widely used in the PR profession. So is *Gebbie's.* Both give editors' names and list media that *do,* as well as those that *do not,* accept advertising. A newsletter or journal may not accept ads but may be extremely valuable in terms of publicity exposure opportunities.

Ayer's Directory is exceptionally helpful for trying to construct a list of media in a particular city. All the publications in that city are listed alphabetically, along with such essentials as address, editor's name, and circulation.

Specialized directories for states and some cities are also published (e.g., *New York City Publicity Outlets).*

Whether to develop one's own media list or go to a computerized list house is a matter of personal preference. Some companies and PR firms like to develop their own lists, while others find they have little time for that and turn to computerized services that also offer a press release mailing service.

Whether to address press releases to editors by name or title is another matter of individual choice. There are all sorts of points of view on the issue.

Ideally, if you know the editor personally or if his name is listed in a directory, it would seem logical to address the release to that name and title. In the real world, however, editors change publications, as well as titles at the same publication. To avoid mailroom confusion and to ensure that the release will get to the right party, you should address the editor by title only. This usually holds true even if you know the editor. If you haven't spoken with him very recently, he might have quit or moved to another position. Besides, you will find that addressing editors by title speeds up your own organization's internal handling of press release mailings (unless, of course, you opt to use a computerized mailing service). Address labels that have been previously typed or run off can be used for every envelope. And rubber hand stamps can then be used for specific titles, such as managing editor, computer editor, or business editor.

Repeating the Message

It's worth mentioning again, in the context of communicating with the media, that recasting a release in a different form and sending it out again to the same editor is worth the effort. Look at it from the editor's point of view. In the majority of instances, the publication has on staff an editor whose responsibility is to handle, say, product releases. Because of the abundance of releases he receives (most product editors are literally deluged with them), he is forced to make decisions as to which he'll use for the current issue, which he'll file away for possible future consideration, and which he'll toss.

In his decision-making process, the product editor tries to pick out releases that will be of greatest interest to his readers. The release you send him today may or may not get used, even though it is in someway related to his readers' needs. He may not like the theme of the release or the approach, or he may simply reject it for lack of space, favoring other releases he has received. If you send only one release, the editor's rejection will be final. But that is a disservice to both the editor and the product. At another time, with few releases to choose from, in a different frame of mind, or faced with a different approach, the editor might accept the release.

That is precisely why a company ought to consider submitting different releases, all with different appeals, but about the same product. The editor might just take a liking to one of the approaches, whereupon the release will get into print.

It is conceivable, too, that two (or more) messages about the same product might appeal to the editor. In that case, there is some chance he would run them in successive issues—particularly if the messages are really different. To help the editor do that, he must be furnished with totally different photos or drawings with each version of the release. Each of the photos might depict the particular point covered in the release. Since product editors often prefer a picture (photo or drawing) that illustrates the editorial angle, they probably would object to using a photo they previously used, even though the message is different.

It is important to emphasize that the publicist who submits multiple releases is not trying to trick a busy editor into not recognizing a release he has already run—or rejected. Quite the contrary. There may be legitimate reasons for an editor to run more than one release on the same product at different times—or to run a release now after having rejected one on the same product for a previous issue of the same publication.

The product application release, for example, offers an opportunity not usually offered by a product feature release—an opportunity to interest editors of *vertically*-oriented publications. Circulated to their own specific industries, these publications provide excellent outlets for application releases pertaining to those industries. A case in point is the car-laundry timer mentioned in Chapter 2. The timer release might be aimed at publications reaching manufacturers and end users of car laundering equipment. Seeing that the release specifically addresses the needs of their readers, editors would be more apt to run it in preference to a more general product feature release not slanted specifically for their audience. In all likelihood, horizontal publications (those cutting across all industries) would also be interested in a specific-application release.

By distributing both features- and applications-oriented release to the media, you significantly increase your chances for exposure in any one publication. You also increase the probability of obtaining multiple exposure for your product in the *same* publication (in the same or different issues), as well as increase the total number of publications running the release.

The Payoff

An integral aspect of distributing product releases to the media is knowing if they get used. There are several ways companies and PR practitioners can find this out. For one, many trade publications print a reader service or "bingo card" number below each product mention, which is matched on the reader service post card bound into the magazine. Seeking information about a product, the reader circles the appropriate number on the self-addressed, postage-paid reader service card and mails it back to the magazine. The publisher, in turn, compiles a list of responses during a particular period and mails it—often as a computer printout—to the company. In addition to knowing who inquired about the product, the company also knows for sure that the release was used by the publication. It discovers which magazines "pull" best for a particular product and, on that basis, chooses publications for its advertising media list.

But some magazines do not provide bingo cards. And some readers respond late, after they've seen an ad or additional publicity about the product, or not at all. In such instances, there may be no evidence that a publication ran the release. With newspapers, there is no reader service number, and the consumer's only opportunity to respond is to buy the product at a retail outlet. And again, the product manufacturer has no way of knowing that the release actually appeared.

Some might argue that knowing where the release ran isn't important, so long as it brings results. But, for PR purposes, sales aren't enough. The diligent PR practitioner will want to know not only which media are running his releases, but also which are eliciting positive responses. Finding that a publication runs none of the releases sent it over a period of time might justify a call to the publication to see if there are any special or unusual editorial requirements.

Another reason for knowing when a release appears in print is that PR programs are frequently judged by companies on the basis of the number of media that run the release—not necessarily on results. As a defense mechanism of sorts for the PR practitioner, then, it is important to be able to produce on demand a comprehensive list showing where the releases appeared.

Probably the most important reason for knowing if and where releases appear is company-centered: To show prospects and others that the product is getting exposure in various media. A high response demonstrates to salespeople that their company is doing something to help them sell; to the retailer that the company is trying to promote the product to his potential customers; to the prospective purchaser that the product has garnered editorial notice; and to the financial community that the company is succeeding, which, in turn, helps the company raise capital when necessary. The fact that the release has obtained multimedia exposure can be effectively demonstrated to a company's various publics by running off product-mention clippings on an office copier or by making offset reprints of the publicity.

Beyond the indirect methods noted above, how does one assess release usage? Phoning an editor to ask if he ran the release is definitely not advisable. If everyone who sent him a release followed up with a phone call, he'd have no time to do anything else. Needless to say, this is a good way to irritate an editor—to the point where he may automatically reject future releases you send his way.

USING A CLIPPING SERVICE

The best method for determining product release exposure is to retain one or more press clipping services. Some of them are particularly efficient at finding publicity mentions that appear in trade publications and consumer media. Some clipping services specialize in publications on a nationwide basis, while others clip only their own regionals. Some even provide clips of radio and TV exposures. Bacon's, Burrelle's, and Luce are three top clipping services.

There are a few drawbacks connected with clipping services. While they do a remarkable job in general, they nevertheless miss quite a few releases. You will detect that fact when two services are clipping for the same items. While many of the clips they send you will be duplicates, some will not—which means that each service is picking up publicity appearances that the other is missing.

There is really no way to remedy the situation. Letters and phone calls to the service result in promises to try harder. But experience with these services shows that the same thing keeps happening. What can be most frustrating is that they sometimes pick up the insignificant clips from minor publications and fail to send you major clips from the multimillion-circulation giants. And that can undermine a publicist's attempts to impress company management with the effectiveness of his product publicity program. Fortunately, many of the major appearances are detected by friends, sales personnel, customers, office clerks, and spouses, who bring them to the attention of management. All you can do is pray that this will happen to your overlooked clips.

Obviously, trying to unearth publicity appearances by yourself is a losing battle. You might be able to cover the leading media in a particular field. But even that is tremendously time-consuming, to say nothing of covering all of the publications on a broad-spectrum media list. If you've constructed the media list carefully and properly, it ought to contain a sizable number of publications—far too many to try to read yourself or even to assign to an assistant to read. It is better, by far, to assign the job to a clipping service—and to more than one if you want to play it safe and minimize the misses.

Another shortcoming of clipping services is the time lag between their response and the appearance of an item. Granted, they will spot it in *The New York Times* and send it to you in a few days. But you may wait weeks, even months, before you receive a clipping that appeared in the *Rag Picker Gazette*. The more remote a publication is from the mainstream of readers and industries, the longer it takes before you get a clipping from it. Clips from smaller-circulation publications also seem to take longer.

It is worth noting that, once retained, clipping services do not automatically clip what you expect them to. While you may be looking for clips that salespeople can use as selling aids (e.g., significant writeups about the product), what you may get instead are listings of exhibitors at a particular trade show. To some, that kind of clip may be important. Strategically, however, it serves little, if any, purpose. Nevertheless, you will probably be flooded with such listings clips (and pay dearly for each one) unless you advise the clipping service that "listings" are not what you've retained them for.

Fortunately, clipping services are very good about clipping only what you ask them to. However, you must be precise. If your order is ambiguous, you stand to be inundated with clips that may be totally irrelevant to your effort. If you just want them to clip all mentions of the company name, tell them so. If not, be sure to specify exactly what you want—and what you don't want. For example, you may want clippings of the company name only when it is used in conjunction with the product you are interested in. You may also want to clip mentions of company people, regardless of whether their name is used along with that of the company. If so, the names of those you want clipped must be given to the clipping service as part of your order (which can be amended and updated from time to time).

PUTTING THE CLIPS TO WORK

In spite of the few weaknesses of the clipping services, they are a significant element in a strategic PR program. Any company that feels it can do without such a service is probably not serious about its PR. It is up to the PR practitioner to convince management of the importance of the service. Failing to do so will usually put the PR program at a decided disadvantage.

A major consideration on the part of management in the decision to employ a clipping service is the ultimate use of the clips. There are those who receive clips, admire them, possibly flaunt them before a few close associates, and stuff them into a drawer where they may remain for years. But this is a serious mistake. As we've seen, press clippings have all sorts of strategic uses, perpetuating the initial appearance of the item or article in a newspaper or magazine.

When a publicity mention appears in a publication, its audience is rather limited. Advertising agencies are familiar with studies of how many readers of a magazine see their ad in any one issue—certainly far fewer than the total number of readers. And the same holds for publicity. Yet, the audience that might still see the item, benefit by it, and act on it is vastly greater than the readers of any one publication.

For that reason, anyone taking his PR seriously should do everything possible to make that publicity work for him—over and over again.

As a morale-builder, publicity about a company or its products ranks high in giving employees a feeling that their company is recognized and respected by the outside world. To foster that feeling, bulletin boards and company publications are ideal vehicles for displaying news items about the company and its products to company employees.

The principals of a company often entertain important visitors in their offices: Securities analysts, customers, vendors, government officials, and representatives of the press. A finely bound scrapbook of company clippings would provide a casual, yet impressive way to convey the stature of the company to these visitors.

Sales personnel are continually seeking legitimate excuses to drop in on a prospect. In many instances, the product or service they sell offers them nothing new to talk about. Still a visit to the prospect would be worthwhile—if only to reinforce previous meetings and renew relationships. The fact that the prospect might be interested in seeing the news items provides a perfect excuse for a visit.

Again, the salesperson welcomes *batches* of clippings—possibly run off on an office copier—to show prospective customers how frequently editors are mentioning the company and its products—an indication of the company's importance. To furnish salespeople with such ammunition, it's often useful to wait until a sizable quantity of clips accumulate. (With a normally active PR program, that usually does not take very long.) Then the clips can be copied, either singly or in groupings, on an 8-1/2″ × 11″ sheet and stapled together in batches. Such a sheaf of reproduced clippings is quite impressive, providing something of substance to flash before a prospect.

Then, too, clippings can be dramatically reproduced as part of a printed mailing piece and distributed to an entire prospect list, the theme being that editors are talking about the product. To an industrial or commercial prospect, that demonstrates quite credibly the product's significance. To a retailer, it shows that there is media exposure to attract store traffic.

Clippings can also be enlarged and used as trade-show booth backdrops. Demonstrating media exposure and implying editorial endorsement, the clippings say more in terms of product significance than any enlarged product photo. They also remind exhibit visitors of publicity about the products they've already seen in publications they've read.

For public companies, clippings or reproductions of them mailed to underwriters, securities analysts, and brokerage houses provide important and impressive news about the company. The clippings can be used by analysts as a source of credible information and by brokerage houses as a means of demonstrating the kind of company they are recommending to their customers for investment. Even nonpublic companies would do well to demonstrate to private backers and investors that the company is significant enough to be continually referred to in the media.

Part Two

REACTIVE PR

7

Developing a VR Program

In this section of the book, we are going to be employing the various PR vehicles we discussed in the first section. For the most part, we'll be using them as elements in reactive (as opposed to proactive) strategies.

Before plunging headlong into strategies, however, it is important to determine what information is needed for formulating them. That determination is ordinarily accomplished at the beginning of the development of a PR program by means of the communications audit. However, the traditional audit, as we described it in Chapter 1, can be seriously inadequate for the purposes of vulnerability relations, or VR. Insofar as it involves only a search for opportunities, it can lock a company into a public relations program that is only partially effective. PR should nearly always be supplemented by VR.

Limitations of the Traditional Audit

We've seen that the audit usually involves interrogating the marketing executives of a company on objectives, products or services, and markets for the coming year. All too often, however, the audit fails to yield the kind of information that is really needed. Frequently, the information forthcoming from company executives resembles a "wish" list. That is, those who are audited come up with a series of wish-fulfillment responses to audit questions: What they would *like* to happen in the short and long terms; what markets they would *like* to enter; how much they would *like* to increase sales.

Unfortunately, the wish list is often the sole basis for an otherwise well-intentioned PR program. However, it falls far short of providing the facts required for waging strategic warfare against unrelenting competitors. The information that is indispensable to a strategically oriented marketing PR program includes actual and potential problems—as well as opportunities. That is, the program must be based on a thorough examination of external circumstances over which a company has no control: Consumer attitudes, economic conditions, government policies, and competitive activities. These circumstances can generate problems, and these problems can make it difficult or impossible to achieve the objectives on the wish list.

Essentially, the problems derive from prospective customers' fears about doing business with a company—fears that either arise by themselves; at the instigation of competitors; or as a result of political, economic, and social changes.

Unless the objectives that are drawn up at an audit fully take into account a company's vulnerabilities—the risks (real, imagined, or rumored) that the company represents to those with whom it has business relationships—a PR plan based on those objectives is relatively ineffective against a major competitor whose strategy feeds on those vulnerabilities.

At this point, it might be useful to find out whether these vulnerabilities can be countered as effectively through advertising as through PR.

Of course, advertising and public relations can be used to communicate identical messages. However, as we've seen, advertising lacks third-party endorsement. Regardless of message content, consumers consider advertising to be the voice of a company talking about itself.

Public relations brings to the battlefield third-party reactions —often from well-respected editors and spokesmen who are in no way connected with the company and have nothing to gain or lose by their implicit or explicit endorsements. For that reason, PR is generally regarded as being more credible than advertising.

To be sure, once credibility is established, advertising can be effective. However, because of its lack of credibility, advertising alone cannot overcome a company's vulnerabilities. There are so many types of vulnerabilities that an advertising budget directed against all of them would probably be rapidly dissipated. For this reason, advertising should be used to convince specific markets of product or service benefits. PR should be used to reenforce product claims, to counteract vulnerabilities, and to bolster confidence in the company on the part of prospective customers and other important publics.

About Vulnerabilities

In essence, vulnerabilities are alleged or actual weaknesses in a company, its products, or its operations that can affect its relationships with its publics. When vulnerabilities actually exist, the smartest thing a company can do is face up to them and try to correct them. Frequently, however, the vulnerabilities are simply imagined or suspected by prospective customers and others. Or they are invented by a competitor's sales team to cast a company in a bad light and make it easier for competition to win out in the marketplace.

Consider that last possibility. We've all teethed on the old saw that it's not good practice to criticize your competitors. Theoretically, customers discount such criticism because it may be self-serving and therefore biased. In the real world, however, criticism can stick, especially if it is repeated often enough. Like a statement made in a courtroom by a lawyer or a witness, it may be ruled inadmissible, and the judge may order it stricken from the record. Yet, as lawyers know, the statement may leave an indelible mark on the jury and thereby influence its judgment.

It's the same with company-related matters. An injurious allegation may be either expressed or implied. Either way, it might be remembered by prospective customers to the extent that it neutralizes an otherwise effective advertising or sales promotion campaign.

As an example—a particularly vicious one in this case—a major electronics company lost its top executive team in a tragic fire. Yet the company valiantly managed not only to survive, but to fight its way back to its former position as a significant force in its industry. Nevertheless, as the media discovered and reported some time later, the company's competitors tried to take advantage of the situation by suggesting that the company was sinking rapidly and would not survive. Those competitors were making the company seem vulnerable. And they made doing business with the company seem risky.

All too frequently, a company's supposed vulnerabilities lie dormant and unspoken in the prospect's mind, festering there until it's time to place an order. Then their full impact comes to the fore and the order goes to the competition.

What do we know about vulnerabilities? For one thing, they are difficult to pry out of a prospect. They exist in the recesses of the mind. Yet, real or imaginary, these images can render a company helpless. They can have an effect that lingers interminably and becomes an invisible obstacle to sales.

Unearthing Vulnerabilities

Why is it that information about vulnerabilities doesn't show up during a marketing communications audit? The answer is simple. It's because those who could furnish such information—the salespeople—are normally absent from the audit. Traditionally included at such a meeting are sales and marketing executives and similar senior-level company officials. Some of them may be remote from the problems salespeople encounter in their daily rounds. Others may be unaware that communications programs must take a company's vulnerabilities into account. They see no reason to provide PR or advertising people with the sort of information that can be used in countering such vulnerabilities.

A problem may even stem from the PR person who is conducting the audit. He may be intimidated by the company's executives who rush him through the audit and proffer only the kind of information *they* feel he needs for the PR program. Such intimidation may arise whether the PR practitioner is on the staff of the company or is part of an outside organization—an advertising agency or PR firm. As an "outsider," he may not want to push a client too far for fear of jeopardizing his relationship and possibly the account itself.

The only sure-fire way to obtain the necessary facts, is to get them from the people who are out in the field—the company's salespeople. In my experience, the best information of this type most often comes from them. They are privy to a wealth of reactions and responses from prospective customers—which often fail to reach the ears of top executives.

Sometimes, these field people withhold such information from those they report to for fear it will discredit them. And even when they report it, their regional supervisors may neglect to pass it on. Instead, they may push the salespeople all the harder to overcome these negative reactions. They fail to realize that the reactions are based on their prospects' almost unconscious fears which are extremely difficult to allay without a PR or VR program designed to overcome them.

The best method of getting this valuable information is to spend time with the company's salespeople, who acquire it in spite of their tight-lipped prospective customers by "networking." Salespeople network naturally. They enjoy exchanging ideas and experiences with their peers at trade shows, on trains and planes, and at motels where they tend to congregate after a day's rounds. And part of what they exchange is information about problems— particularly with competitors and consumers. Spend a relaxed, casual day or two with these salespeople and this information will begin to surface. You will also hear the salespeople's views of company policies and management practices that may be demoralizing to the sales organization. That information, too, should be taken into account in the PR program, since a large factor in selling is keeping a company's sales organization contented.

Information of both types is readily obtainable. When I was fresh out of college and in my first PR job, I was sent by a client— a paint manufacturer—to Charlotte, North Carolina, and spent a couple of days going from dealer to dealer with a local salesman. In those two days, that salesman revealed more dealer problems than I believe the company's marketing people ever imagined existed. In addition, problems in company-salesman relationships came to light—problems that were injuring the company's sales efforts not just in North Carolina, but nationwide. All that was unearthed by a PR neophyte, indicating how really easy it is to come by such invaluable information when an audit is extended beyond the confines of company headquarters.

Even without conducting the type of audit described here, the

PR practitioner can develop strategies for most types of vulnerabilities. That's because most companies are susceptible to very nearly the same kinds of vulnerabilities. However, if a thorough audit is not conducted, it will be difficult to justify the investment required to counter vulnerabilities. Without concrete evidence that a particular vulnerability exists, management may resist budgeting for a VR strategy to counteract it. The audit, then, becomes a necessary component in convincing management that certain vulnerabilities constitute a real problem and that PR time and effort should be spent on solving it.

The "Working Backwards" Exercise

Let's assume that, after doing its homework, the PR team has convinced management that certain vulnerabilities exist—real or rumored—and that management has agreed PR should be used to counteract them. What now?

To help answer that question, the second half of this book will take up a variety of vulnerability situations and suggest specific strategies for handling them. Becoming aware of a company's vulnerabilities is one thing; dealing with them is something else. It takes some creativity and a good deal of experience. But how do we gain experience while the meter is running and the company or client is paying the freight?

Fortunately, practice situations are all around us, particularly in newspapers and consumer and trade publications. The trick is to read an article or item that deals in some way with a company or organization and then work backwards to discover if the item might have been part of a VR-type strategy. This involves imagining what vulnerability situation might have inspired the piece. That is, we fantasize that it's really part of a VR maneuver.

Underscore the word "fantasize." In all probability, the company written up in the article or news item had no such vulnerability. That is, you'll be imagining everything. However, the practice is valuable because it will encourage you to think along strategic PR lines.

Besides exercising your mind, working backwards can also help you to accumulate an arsenal of PR strategies. You try to figure out what public relations problem might be behind a particular story. And once you think you've figured it out, you'll have something to add to your store of PR techniques that might prove useful in a similar situation with your own company or client.

Let's see how working backwards is done. The example referred to below turned up in a popular daily newspaper read by managers and entrepreneurs. It illustrates how a clever PR person might try to counter rumors about a company's functional situation.

In this instance, the story was an interesting educational piece written to demonstrate what a financial vice president does for his company—what his daily routine consists of. In all likelihood, the story was what it appeared to be and nothing more—an attempt to give readers some insight into an interesting and little understood occupation. But it is just possible that the company mentioned in the piece conceived of this approach as an indirect way of putting down some harmful gossip about it in the industry. There's no way of knowing for sure.

In this particular case, the staff writer noted that one of the functions of a financial vice president is to induce a variety of banks and other financial institutions to lend operating capital to his company. The writer went on to relate how successful this company's financial officer had been in obtaining such loans, even naming banks and institutions that provided the financing.

To the average reader of the publication, the article was nothing more than an informative piece—just like others appearing there regularly. However, for someone accustomed to using PR in vulnerability situations, the article could have been much more.

Just suppose that the company named in the article had been having difficulty convincing prospective customers of its financial stability. Competition might have been talking openly about the company's difficulty in locating funding for its new product line or its R&D operation. And just suppose that, because of this rumor, prospective customers felt that doing business with that company was too risky and that dealing with its competitors would be safer.

Aware of that situation, the company would have been well advised to develop a strategy for demonstrating its success in locating financing—without coming right out and saying it. The trick in such cases is to make the strategy so undetectable that nobody can guess its true intent. That's where creativity comes in.

But why an article in a prestigious publication aimed at top-level executives? That's "obviously" part of the VR strategy, too. If a company can borrow large sums, its credit must be good. And if its credit is good, it must be stable enough to justify a sizable purchase of its products involving long-term delivery and service commitments—that is, the kind of purchase only a top-level executive can authorize. Such a high-level audience would be particularly hesitant about making a long-term arrangement with a vendor who might be financially unstable.

Another aspect of this strategy is the way the article was by-lined. As we've seen, an article by-lined by an executive extolling his own company's financial resources lacks credibility. Plainly, it smacks of propaganda. However, credibility can be attained if a third party tells of the company's financial successes—particularly if the one doing the telling has the backing of a highly regarded publication.

Suppose a prospective customer is considering purchasing from you a machine that is indispensable to its manufacture of a new product that will be ready for market in, say, two years. That's the amount of time it will take you to get the machine produced, installed in your customer's plant, and turning out product. But what if you are giving off signals that you are financially unstable and may not get sufficient credit to buy parts for the machine you are building for your customer. If you can't buy parts, you will delay your customer's introduction of his new product. And the delay could put his company in an unfavorable competitive position. The suspicion that such a situation exists—whether actual or alleged—could deal a severe blow to your own sales efforts. Your prospective customer would certainly be wise to seek out a more stable, less risky vendor.

It is evident, then, that purchases involving large outlays of capital can be swung in one direction on another or rumor alone. It is also evident that a single, creative PR idea has the power to alter the situation dramatically.

Having worked this example backwards and fantasized a VR strategy out of what may have been an innocuous article in a newspaper, you now have a strategy that might be applicable in a similar situation. For that reason alone, it's useful to practice this technique—reading articles and news items and working them backwards to find a possibly hidden VR strategy intended to solve a sticky vulnerability problem. Once you're on to that strategy, you have one more to store away in your own files for future use. And even if you never use it, it's good practice in being creative— something for which this field has an unquenchable need.

8

Two Approaches

We'll begin our exploration of vulnerabilities—and strategies to overcome them—by examining two approaches that apply to every PR vehicle and nearly every PR problem. The first approach will enhance your chances for gaining media exposure for your client or company. The second will increase your ability to survive in tough competitive situations.

The Art of Being Indirect

As we've seen, although everyone knows that companies send out articles and releases primarily for publicity purposes, editors will accept them if they are newsworthy. To make them more acceptable, therefore, they should be written in the form of news stories, rather than sales messages. The best way to accomplish this is to communicate the publicity message *indirectly*. That is, the stories should appear to be reports instead of advertisements. If possible, they should purportedly be about something other than the company or its products. The ostensible message should be used to set the stage for the real message. Sometimes this can be done by using the company as an example illustrating the point made in the story. Let's see how this technique can be applied.

In the case of one high-technology company, the prospects seemed anything but bright for gaining business-section exposure in a major, mass-circulation newspaper. But working backwards, as we've done before, we can see how this firm was able to get its story told.

The company, small and barely on the threshold of being successful, apparently wanted to publicize its success in gathering substantial backing from venture capitalists. It may also have wanted to show how large its order backlog was (as a measure of success).

The item that appeared, however, focused on how any young and budding company goes about getting venture capital and how such a company manages to attract high-level, competent employees away from larger, more successful, and more established firms. That theme, which interested the business editor of a major city newspaper, provided the company's management with an opportunity—using the company as an example—to reveal who its major customers were, how experienced its executives were, how advanced its products were, and who its backers were. The company's claim that it was financially sound gained credibility because—as the article showed—major companies had seen fit to lend it substantial sums of money.

In other words, getting exposure for a how-to-do-it theme at the same time gathered exposure for a more self-serving theme: How *we* did it. Although the approach was indirect, the article touched on every important strength of the company. The story might also have struck back at other companies, large or small, that were openly or covertly downplaying the firm's R&D successes and financial stability to prospective customers.

On another occasion, I came across an item about a company executive's unusual hobby. Working backwards, I realized that the article could possibly be a vehicle for gaining widespread publicity for his company. Although the story ostensibly was about the hobby, it also contained information about the company, its products, and the executive. It was also a clever way of getting a business message into a publication that normally did not publish business or industrial articles—but one whose readers might, in their workaday life, be potential factors in the decision to purchase the kind of product made by the company mentioned in the article. The story might also have been meant to discredit rumors about the caliber of the company's management people.

Seeing a trade magazine article about a company's market research study of a particular product category suggested to me that the company might have had something else up its sleeve. The article demonstrated that research is an important key to successful marketing. To me, however, the article said that the company wanted to demonstrate its success in developing products to meet specific consumer demands. The story might have been planted as a means of countering statements made by competition that the company was trying to foist products onto retailers for which there was little or no demand and that they would wind up stocking their shelves with unsalable merchandise.

When a product may have a difficult time gaining exposure in important consumer-type media, sometimes a tie-in with an organization of some kind solves the problem. I've found that the Boy Scouts and Girl Scouts are particularly cooperative, since they are seeking publicity for themselves, too. In one instance, my client had developed a new fireplace tool that made log-lifting much easier. It was no simple matter, however, to publicize such a limited-appeal product in the consumer press. So I had my client offer to donate several of his fireplace tools to a Girl Scout camp in exchange for photos of the Scouts using them. The Girl Scouts agreed. The widely used story that resulted told how girls from the city learned about outdoor life and camping. But it also showed how the girls used special equipment, like the log-lifting tool. The tie-in with the outside organization provided a vehicle that allowed the product to be brought in indirectly. In this case, the product also received an implied endorsement by the well-known organization using it.

Another client of mine was moving its headquarters to a different town. In itself, such a story usually warrants extremely limited mention in trade and local news media. Sometimes, a photo of the new headquarters building is shown, but little more.

To try for a sizable feature article, I attempted a different approach—interviewing the mayor and community planning director of the town to which my client was moving. I asked them about methods they used to attract my client's company and other businesses to their community—the incentives offered and the reasons for offering them. Then I produced a feature article that showed how a community goes about upgrading itself by attracting high-caliber companies. My client represented an example of companies that met the strict standards set by the town. Thus, the article showed the company off in the best possible way, emphasizing its international scope, as well as other positive attributes. Reprints of the articles proved very valuable when prospective customers asked for literature about the company. They offered a highly credible third-party endorsement of this highly regarded firm.

In another use of indirect PR, a well-known company showed how, because of a new law, it was able to defer its earnings until the following year when taxes would be lower, while declaring its expenses in the current higher-tax-rate year. Ostensibly a how-to piece in the financial area, the article appeared in a major business publication. However, it might have been intended to tell retailers that they could delay payments for a month at year's end—thus giving them another month's use of their money by doing business with the company referred to in the article.

If the company had addressed retailers directly (which may or may not have been its intention), the message might not have gotten more than marginal exposure in a few industry publications, instead of full coverage in a widely read business magazine. Of particular interest here is that, in place of the usual information about product, quality, pricing, and sales successes, the story dealt with a new tax law situation favoring retailers—a creative way, indeed, to get a message across to retail management.

Another example of the indirect approach was an article written by an advertising agency describing how agencies should select top executives—a how-to piece. Appearing in a publication read by prospective agency clients, it not only described how to conduct the screening process, but also managed to show that the agency (using itself as an example) used these techniques during its own recent high-growth period. Wouldn't it be interesting if the *real* purpose of the article was to show prospective clients that the agency was "hot" and successful and, as a result, had recently added lots of top-flight executives to its staff? Again, the approach was indirect. Perhaps the article was dreamed up to counter innuendos by competition that the agency was slipping or that it hadn't added any worthwhile accounts for quite some time.

The creative approaches cited in the foregoing examples rely on indirectness to interest editors. Normally, if they are creative enough, indirect methods gain greater exposure than do direct ones. Furthermore, because they can use human-interest stories as a vehicle, these methods often result in placements in the mass media—newspaper, consumer magazines, TV, and radio.

Sometimes, the story angle fails to interest a medium whose audience is of value to the company. That was the case with a company that moved to another community. The article appeared not in a publication aimed at the company's prospective customers, but in one whose audience consisted of town and city officials. Was the effort wasted because the audience reading the story meant little or nothing to the company involved? Not necessarily. In some cases, the only exposure possible may be in a medium reaching the "wrong" audience. Yet the right audience can still be affected by it. Even in a wrong publication, the article still has the credibility of a third-party endorsement. And this endorsement can be communicated to other audiences through reprints. If reprints are used as clip-ons to accompany sales letters or proposals or are handed out at trade shows or during sales calls, the parties receiving them will most likely be influenced just as positively as if they were reading the article in one of their own industry publications. The effect of editorial endorsement seems to be that powerful, no matter where it is bestowed. Therefore, if the media addressing your markets reject your article, your next best bet is to find a medium that will accept it. Then, after it's published, reprint it.

The Outfoxing-the-Fox Approach

Fiction writers refer to different types of plots by descriptive names, one of which is the "biter-bit" plot. Essentially, this plot is based on *getting even*. First, the villain does something detrimental to the hero or heroine. Second, the attempt boomerangs and the villain becomes the fall guy. That is, the one who initiated the biting ends up getting bitten.

This kind of plot can be enacted in real life between companies. For example, your competition is making you look bad and making himself look good. However, you know he is just as vulnerable as you are. So you find a way of discrediting him or refuting what he is saying about you.

THE SQUIRREL EFFECT

Competition's ability to succeed with this strategy depends on his credibility. Possibly, through years of good public relations, he has so convinced the markets and media of his strengths that it is hard to believe otherwise. That is what every company should strive for: to build up an investment in credibility over a span of time so it will pay dividends during lean periods. You might call it the "squirrel effect." A company squirrels away its acorns of public confidence, building up an immense store of these valuable-as-gold nuggets. Then, when something goes wrong, the public will find it hard to believe—even when competition blows the whistle.

That's precisely how a PR program, assiduously implemented year after year, can help a company ride out a storm. It also enables a company to bite back at competitors who can be pushed off the offensive and onto the defensive track through a biter-bit strategy.

When a major competitor of yours is finally cashing in on his store of credibility to your company's detriment—despite his own vulnerability—the time is ripe for you to play a similar game. It makes no sense to stand idly by and watch your competitor erode your market. Counterattacking simply requires the application of tactics that are best described under the banner of vulnerability relations.

Of course, the longer you've been applying these techniques or tactics, the easier it is for you to counterattack effectively.

How this thrust and counter-thrust strategy works can be seen particularly well in an example involving a high-technology industry. In this case, only a limited number of small, new companies have entered the market; most of those already there are divisions of long-established giants. Because the industry is relatively new and involved in high-technology work, R&D is at a feverish pace.

AN EASY CREDIBILITY

The divisions of companies that have already established their credibility have few qualms about announcing publicly that they've made specific breakthroughs or advances that will be introduced commercially and have applications in certain fields—even though the introduction may still be many months off.

Part of their strategy is to cite specific areas of application and to direct announcements to the vertical media servicing those areas. Now here's the rub. Although the verticals are generally sophisticated enough about their own industry's technology, they may have little knowledge of the technical area announced—either because the technology is new or because it is new in their fields. Unable to critique the development as knowledgeably and thoroughly as they should, the editors may publish the company's announcement simply because it affects their fields.

Chalk one up for competition.

What gives the announcement even greater credibility, although the technology is new to the industry, is the company's already-established name. Here is where a new product can benefit from the store of credibility that a company has built up over the years.

Because the announcement is made by a known company, audiences affected by it assume that the new development will soon be on the market. For this reason, they can ignore similar offerings from lesser-known companies who may have only recently come on the scene. That is exactly what the better-known company counts on. Because the technology is new, prospective customers reason that it is safer to wait to do business with a recognized company than to take a chance on an unknown.

What prospective customers don't know is that the better-known company may only be bluffing. Well-entrenched companies sometimes have an uncanny sixth sense in knowing when they can get away with a bluff—and just what kind they can get away with. It's like a poker game. The big winner has all the other players believing he can do no wrong. Then he goes ahead, with no cards at all, and bluffs his way through.

Like the poker winner, well-known companies frequently get away with their bluffs—even with editors. After all, supported by high credibility, bluffs can be hard to beat.

THE SELF-STYMIE

What makes the bluff even more effective is that lesser-known competitors often just lie down and let themselves get trampled on. Their engineers and scientists, frequently in awe of the larger competitors' capabilities, half-believe that what Mr. Big is saying might very well be true (even though logic may say it can't be). They also are afraid of getting themselves and their companies into hot water if they refute Mr. Big's announcement as a marketing ploy—or of using the same ploy themselves and possibly beating Mr. Big to the punch.

A negative influence can also come from another quarter—the lesser-known company's marketing people. Realizing that their company's credibility is not particularly high, they hesitate at announcing what they know they can't deliver immediately for fear of losing what little credibility they may have. So they say nothing and allow competition to get away with announcing a product that may also be undeliverable.

What most self-stymied strategists fail to grasp is that they risk very little loss of credibility. Anyone with experience in new technology developments knows that there is often a long lag time between announced innovations and implementations—due to any number of unforeseeable events. The fact that a company has faced delays doesn't mean the announcement was a misrepresentation that stands to damage the company's credibility. It merely suggests that because the technology is as yet untried, the wrinkles have to be ironed out before it is ready for market.

Admitting that fact can even make a company look good. In spite of demand for the product, the company refuses to release it until it is confident there will be no problems.

THE COUNTER-STRATEGY

What, then, are the vulnerability-relations tactics that can be used to offset an established company's claims and their implications for your company? And how can you get the jump on the well-established company?

First of all, the company's top management can issue executive-statement releases reporting on the company's progress in the new technology area. However, the company should not try to cover all the details in a single release. By parceling out the information in a series of releases, the company will be able to gain repeated media exposure and impact its markets over and over again.

One type of release that is particularly useful in beating Mr. Big to the punch is an announcement that your company is on the verge of a major new development. Although it mentions no specifics, the release has tremendous impact—particularly in an industry in which there are few competitors or in which everyone knows to some degree what the others are working on (in which case, the news may come as a shock to competitors). A side benefit from this approach is that it tells editors that your company is one they ought to keep an eye on—regardless of how quiet you've been up to now. Still another benefit is that the release can stop prospective customers from irrevocably deciding to wait for Mr. Big's product introduction and to refrain from buying until then. And it can induce prospects to get in touch with your sales organization to squeeze out additional information. As a result, your sales people will have an opportunity to begin building potential-customer relationships long before you have something concrete to sell them.

One word of caution, however. *Sooner or later, your company had better come up with the kind of development you've been making statements about.* If not, you can kiss your credibility goodbye for a long time.

A hard-to-beat way of outdoing competition is to announce your new development at a press briefing. A notch below a press conference in psychological impact, a briefing makes a bid for media exposure without appearing to pull out all the stops. Attending the briefing, in addition to media representatives, could be customers, prospects and—if the company is public or planning to go that route—securities analysts.

A word about additional invitees to the briefing. Generally, it is poor practice to mix editors with people of other interests. The press may get miffed at the commercialism and at the nonmedia questions. Also, trade press editors, savvy about what's going on in their own industry, may comment unflatteringly about your development and negatively influence a prospective customer's decision to purchase. The way to get around this is to stage the briefing (or press conference) as a two-parter. For example, in the morning, the event might be strictly for media; in the afternoon, for everybody else.

The same words of caution mentioned earlier about verge-of-announcement news releases apply to press briefings: The new development had better come soon—or else. You can rationalize product unavailability by saying that mass production details have yet to be worked out or that a few design or theoretical problems remain to be solved. Either claim buys additional time for R&D without losing face—valuable time when competition is threatening to beat you to your market by using the same ploys. And it makes competition look a little foolish and less credible if they've been telling everyone that they're miles ahead of your company.

Clearly, then, there is no reason to stand by and let equally vulnerable competitors make you look vulnerable in the eyes of your various publics. This holds for the particular vulnerability of being behind them in development of a new product or technology —or for any of the other vulnerabilities described in this book. Again, if competititon has nurtured its credibility and stored it away for a long period of time, then he stands a reasonably good chance of winning the game. However, your chances for success are much improved if you've learned what you can do for your credibility in both the long and short runs.

9

Starting Out

It may be human nature to pull for anyone starting out in a new and possibly difficult direction. In the business world, however, starting out can become the source of a vulnerability that competitors may be able to use to their advantage.

In this chapter, we'll explore various ways of starting out, the vulnerabilities to which they expose a company, and methods of overcoming them using VR strategies.

The "Newcomer" Vulnerability

One starting-out situation involves breaking into a new market. In such circumstances, it is not unusual for competition to intimate that the company, new to the market, is inexperienced in the field and hasn't established a track record sufficient to justify a substantial order. This can happen even to companies over a century old, with extensive marketing experience. If the company or its product is unknown in the new market, competition might point out to prospective customers the dangers of doing business with such newcomers. As a result, would-be customers, unaware of this competitive strategy, might opt to deal with companies they know better. Despite extensive advertising, promotion, and product publicity directed at the new market, fears about the newcomer, possibly initiated by competition, could nullify the entire marketing effort.

Companies encountering this problem must do everything possible to overcome the negative aspects of a newcomer image—

but not by denying that they are a newcomer. Denying the fact does little more than open the door wider for competition to march in with the "truth" and thereby capitalize on the "cover-up."

What bona fide newcomers can do to combat such tactics will be discussed later in this chapter. Meanwhile, a brief look at two case histories will be instructive. One newcomer company was in the building products field—making dampproofing and caulking compounds, concrete admixtures, and so on. These compounds, typically specified by architects for large projects, can be ordered in huge quantities for, say, a skyscraper that is under construction. In this case, the company happened to be an oldtimer in the field. Its salespeople, however, preferred *not* to call on architects, in spite of the potential for large orders. Their reason was that there was too much lag time between specifying the product and ordering it for the project. Commissions came faster and the salespeople looked better at weekly sales meetings when orders followed quickly on the heels of a sales call. For that reason, the salespeople opted to call on building supply dealers from whom sales, although considerably smaller, came faster.

As a result of this narrowly focused sales activity, the company and its products remained virtually unknown to the architectural community. Competition was quick to cash in on this, virtually labeling the company as an unknown, in spite of the fact that it had been in the business for generations. Although some architects remembered the company from way back, they were easily convinced that it had discontinued making the kinds of products architects typically specified.

With the company's newcomer image massaged by competition, it is easy to see why architects found it more comfortable to fall back on ordering from what they considered to be the more tried and true companies. This is a fairly typical vulnerability or underdog situation requiring a reactive PR approach to overcome the external influences of competition.

The foregoing was an example of a company seeking to market the same product line—a long-standing one, in fact—to two different markets and coming off as a newcomer in one of them. Such is not always the case. In some instances, the company may be an old one that is well known even in circles in which it doesn't market its products. Yet, it can still come off as a newcomer when it develops a new product for a new market. A multi-billion-dollar aerospace company sought to reposition itself as a manufacturer of products for the automotive, electronics, and other industries, in addition to its aerospace product line. In spite of its well-known name, the company still had to compete with others who were firmly entrenched in those industries. More than that, it had to find ways of overcoming what competition in those industries might have been saying about it and its products—by virtue of its new-comer status.

THE SPONSORED AWARD

As we'll see, there are numerous VR methods for killing the seeds of criticism cleverly planted by competition. One way—successful in many instances—is the *sponsored-award competition*. Eager to gain recognition in a field in which it is little known, a company can sponsor an award for people who have contributed significantly over the past year to the industry or field —be they scientists, engineers, or businessmen. The task of screening and selection can be assigned to a panel consisting of persons who are regarded as industry leaders and authorities. Aside from adding prestige to the award, the reputation of panel members encourages applicants or nominees to submit papers or other documentation of their work. Review by their highly re-garded peers who are on the panel represents an honor few would want to pass up.

Selection of a distinguished panel represents a significant step in drawing attention to the award. But going about it in an industry to which a company is a relative newcomer can be difficult. Just who are the respected names and how can they be approached tactfully and in a way that does not smack of exploitation?

One good source of information is the editors of major trade publications. They know who the industry notables are. Besides, they are accustomed to the sometimes unusual requests of compa-nies marketing their products to the industry. An editor willing to cooperate can be an invaluable aid in making the initial contacts with prospective panelists and sounding out their interest in be-coming part of an awards panel. The editor can then pass along the names of interested parties either to the PR professional or to an executive of the company who, in turn, can directly contact the would-be panelists and sign them up. Verbal agreement by the industry authority to serve as a member of the panel is sometimes adequate. But some written indication—possibly in a letter from him—is preferable, since his name will have to be used later in news releases and articles describing the awards competition.

Once formed, the panel can establish the rules of the competition, the kinds of achievements that will be considered, the mechanics of the screening process, and the manner in which prospective entrants will be notified that the awards competition exists. It is also important to determine where the award will eventually be presented. The panel, knowledgeable in the industry, can provide insight into major industry functions and events. Usually, it is better for a company's award presentation to be part of an already existing and recognized industry event—at least until its award becomes well known. The reason for this is that gaining media exposure requires attendance by editors and reporters. While a new award ceremony might not attract much of a media turnout, an event that is known and respected industry-wide would almost certainly have a captive audience containing a good representation of media people interested in the industry's activities.

Maximizing the company's connection wtih the award is vital to establishing the company's image in the industry. This can be done through releases, interviews with company executives and judges, and feature articles, thereby tracking the awards activities every step of the way. Once a company has everything in place— assurance that the award will become a reality, the panel selected, and details of the competition ironed out—a news release can be issued to the trade and business press announcing the award sponsorship. In certain instances, consumer news media might be appropriate, too. Possibly, another release on the same subject, but quoting an executive of the firm on the competition, can be issued. That could be followed by an announcement of panel member selection, which could be succeeded by a series of releases on entry rules, deadlines, the number of applicants, the number of finalists, a final announcement of time remaining before applications will no longer be accepted for the competition, and an announcement of when and where the winner will be chosen. Distributing a number of releases over a period of time is a way of maximizing exposure opportunities. The event can even be split in two, one part for announcing the winner and the other for awarding a prize to the winner. These latter two events lend themselves readily to news releases, media interviews, and feature articles.

Run on a yearly basis, an awards competition can become an industry event, and the company sponsoring it can shed its reputation as a newcomer.

PERSONNEL ANNOUNCEMENTS

Awards are only one way of getting across the message that a company is not a stranger to an industry, but is an established organization with which others can comfortably and safely do business.

An almost too obvious approach is exposure in *media personnel columns*. These columns are well read by well-established representatives of all industries, who look for the names of people they've known in the industry—possibly one-time co-workers whom they've lost touch with. By establishing the simple routine of giving recognition—possibly by a dinner or even a simple ceremony—to those who have been with the company for a long time, the company can very innocently demonstrate that it has been around for a while. This recognition should be accompanied by news releases directed at the personnel columns of trade publications servicing the industries in question. Once such notices begin appearing regularly, prospective customers in the industry will get the message that the company is not a newcomer, but has been in existence for at least as many years as the employee or employees mentioned in the news item. Photos will capture larger, more viable space for the item.

The simplicity of this approach is evidence that, to be effective, a public relations program need not involve complicated media maneuvers. Often, establishing an easy-to-follow routine—like issuing personnel announcements—can go a long way toward counteracting what the competition might be saying or doing.

EXECUTIVE-STATEMENT RELEASES

Another alternative is the executive-statement approach, described earlier. Because executives who are regularly cited or quoted in the media are usually regarded as people of some distinction or authority and their companies as leaders in the industry, this approach can go a long way toward dispelling the notion that a company is unknown in the industry.

Again, these executive statements must appear frequently because only those executives and companies that are read about on a regular basis tend to be regarded by readers as newsmakers.

As we discussed previously, executive statements need not be focused on the executive's company. Statements about industry practices tend to position the executive even more solidly as someone the media regard as an authority in the field.

Having listed typical executive-statement topics earlier, let us now examine how some of them might be used.

Critiques About Industry Practices. In such critiques, the executive proffers his personal views on any number of topics germane to the industry. The executive can agree or disagree with industry goals, methods, or practices. He can "blue-sky" what he might like to see happen years from now to benefit the industry. The important point is that the reader assumes that the executive was singled out by the publication's editors to voice his views. That in itself rather pointedly marks the executive as a leading figures in the industry—and his company as an important part of the industry.

Short- and Long-Term Industry Forecasts. A topic such as this might turn off an executive because he thinks it requires too much research or compels him to divulge highly confidential information about the industry. However, forecasting need require neither excessive work nor secret-sharing. The executive can make certain prognostications that might be linked with consumer, distributor, supplier, or raw material trends or with marketing strategies that the company or industry is pursuing. He can draw parallels between past, present, and future trends. These can relate to the company's own industry, to markets in general, or to specific markets. In fact, altering the prognostications to suit different specific markets provides an opportunity to slant a news release to each of those markets. A useful practice is to send the same release to every market but to alter the first paragraph of each release to suit each audience. This approach has tremendous editor appeal —particularly when his industry is mentioned in the headline. It also establishes the executive and his company as firmly entrenched entities in a particular industry. If they weren't leaders—the reader surmises—why would their forecast have gotten into print?

It is important to note that forecasts are a pet topic with editors, who often run entire sections on forecasts just prior to or after the new year. Keeping an eye on the publication's editorial calendar will often clue you in to other times that forecasts are being prepared. At those times, executive-statement releases or statements for roundups are usually more than welcome.

Company Activity Forecasts. To help position a company as part of an industry to which it is new, the opening sentences of these releases ought to relate specifically to the industry. The release can then go on to describe industry-related activities: Anticipated marketing ventures, product developments, R&D programs, plant expansions, and so on. One interesting variation on the company forecast is the ''leak'' release, in which an executive might state that his company is on the brink of an important breakthrough, announcement, or innovation. When it is regarded as a leak, an announcement can generate a lot more exposure than would an ordinary release. The editor interest that such a leak might arouse can lead to an interview, and that might lead to anything from a mention to a full-fledged news feature.

It is a good idea to have photos on file of the executive making the statement. Editors who do these interviews—whether in person or over the phone—are often tempted to devote more editorial space to an interview when they can run a photo along with it. In a full-fledged executive-statement program, in which a number of executives from a company make statements regularly, it is good preplanning to ask a local photographer to visit company headquarters and, in a single session, take portrait-type, head-and-shoulder shots of as many executives as possible.

New Technology Appraisals. Appraising a new technology in the industry is a good way for the quoted executive to come off as an authority in, rather than a newcomer to, the industry. Of course, both the editor and the executive know that the former did not *seek out* the opinion of the latter. Instead, the opinion came "over the transom"—via a news release. But once the statement is in print, the difference is impossible to detect. Given enough executive-statement releases that cross the editor's desk from the same company, some are bound to show up in print (which is one reason why a continuous program is important).

The executive statement on new technology in the industry needn't touch on the technology used by the executive's own company. But it should express his views—positive or negative—on the subject. Recently, I issued on behalf of a client an executive-statement release that pointed out how certain technical terms used by others in his industry to describe a new technology were actually misleading. More than being an example of how an executive can offer critiques of current events in his industry, the release proved extremely successful, so whetting editors' appetites that numerous interviews resulted from it.

New Technology Announcements. Publicizing a technological breakthrough in the company via the executive-statement release can be very effective. The breakthrough needn't be major. In fact, an executive—whether marketing or R&D—can even make a statement about a relatively minor innovation or research finding and expound on its implications for either his own company or the industry in general.

In addition to providing an opportunity for exposure in a publication's news section, this type of release demonstrates visibly that the company has an on-going research program. This demonstration is important because it helps to distinguish between what might be regarded as a "garage-type" operation and a legitimate company of more stature, with which a prospective customer needn't fear doing business. For that reason alone, it is evident that the exposure gained may be more valuable than the actual breakthrough or innovation that inspired it.

Views on Federal or State Activities. This type of executive-statement release says much more than the words that go into it. When a company executive takes a stand—be it pro or con—on a governmental issue dealing with his industry, and that stand gets into print, the executive comes off looking like an expert. That is why a point of view on a topic such as this is particularly valuable for a company branded with a newcomer image.

Announcements of New Territories, Appointments, Etc. Low-level, seemingly nonstrategic release announcements help a company maintain continuous exposure in the media and help a company just entering the market gain regular visibility. Cast in the form of an executive statement, however, such releases can accomplish even more.

One example is a release announcing the opening of a new marketing territory or a new office. Such a release is generally written and distributed to the media in a very matter-of-fact way, with little strategic thought, little planning, and very little expectation. However, if it is written not as an announcement, but as an executive-statement release, it can accomplish a good deal more. First, like other executive statements, it will be a candidate for the news section—and therefore far more meaningful in terms of position in the publication than where such announcements normally appear. It will also allow the company to expound somewhat on what the new territory or office means to the company in terms of business prospects, profits, ability to better service customers, and reduced distribution costs to make the product more competitive. The traditional new-office or new-territory announcement never even touches on such subjects and therefore limits what a company can say. The executive-statement release, on the other hand, opens up a number of possibilities—many with powerful strategic overtones. In this disguise, the least-regarded announcement-type release can achieve significant strategic stature.

Similarly, appointment announcements gain in effectiveness when stated by an executive. The usual release covers a new appointee's past work history, his new responsibilities, whom he will be reporting to, his educational background, and so on. Recast as an executive-statement release, it can provide the company with an opportunity to tell, in a strategic way, just what the new appointment means—possibly in terms of an expansion of R&D, a redirection of marketing plans, or an improvement in the company's relationships with vendors or customers. This is a typical VR-type approach that can respond to newcomer and other negative thrusts aimed at a company by competition.

Plant-Openings Announcements. Even if a full-blown plant-opening event is being planned—including attendance by the press, prospects, customers, and government dignitaries—a preliminary statement by a company executive covering many aspects of the new plant and what they will mean competitively gives the company an extra crack at getting media exposure. Like other events, a plant opening provides an opportunity for a one-two punch: A preliminary announcement followed by an announcement of the event when it happens. For most events, there also is an opportunity to "look back" via a press release at what happened, the public's reaction to it, and what is expected to result from it in the future.

Still another way to achieve a non-newcomer image is to gain exposure for the company and its executives side by side with other leading companies and executives in the industry. An excellent way to do that, as pointed out earlier, is by appearing regularly in industry roundup articles. By being cited or quoted alongside leaders, your company appears to prospective customers who read the publication as a leader or force in the industry, too.

But here again, one swallow does not a summer make. Exposure in a single roundup article doesn't convince anyone that a company is an industry leader. On the other hand, lots of editor contact usually pays off with opportunities for participation in numerous roundups.

The "Me-Too" Vulnerability

There's an old saying that everyone has a double somewhere in the world. The same is true of products—only more so. In fact, products in the same category do more than just look alike. They generally function in a similar way, too. For a company just entering a field with a look-alike product, marketing it is far from easy.

Why, after all, would consumers purchase a product that is new to the marketplace when they can purchase one just like it that has been around for some time? Why, too, would a retailer stock a new product with meager promotional backing, if a similar established product is backed by heavy promotion?

These arguments represent the kinds of ploys used by competition to place the newcomer's product in a vulnerable position with prospective customers. Yet the newcomer needn't let himself become an underdog. There are marketing strategies which, coupled with the credibility that PR provides, can turn that company into a tough competitor in the marketplace.

A DIFFERENT BATTLEFIELD

One of the ways this can be achieved is to shift the emphasis from product to nonproduct attributes. As we've seen before, the buyer might be more interested in service—the availability of spare parts, faster delivery, a better operator-training program, or the provision of 24-hour emergency maintenance. Customers might also be impressed by company stability, innovative promotion, or convenient location.

The problem with merely advertising such claims is that sooner or later other companies will join the bandwagon. After all, your competitors, knowing that they must offer more than product alone to win out against you, resort to the very same advertising claims (e.g., 24-hour delivery) as you do.

The result is that everybody goes back to square one. The audience, reading ads run by the various companies, still has nothing to go on to distinguish one product or company from another —since everybody is making the same claims. Seeing them advertised month in and month out, the prospect's eyes soon pass over these repetitious claims that do nothing to convince him that one product is superior to another. In fact, the claims may stop registering in his mind altogether. They become, in effect, "white noise"—meaningless expressions that pass through the mind without making an impact.

Now here is where PR comes in. Any claim can be dramatized in a credible way with PR techniques. It can be acted out, as it were, editorially. Fast delivery, for example, might become the thrust of a feature article about a company that was in a tight spot and was helped immeasurably by speedy emergency delivery. Treated this way, the fast-delivery benefit is more than a mere line of type in an ad. Instead, it is the subject of a feature article that dramatically portrays the benefit of fast delivery to a particular company. Once this claim has been established with credibility, then advertising can drive it home through repetition.

Similar publications, in competition with one another for the advertiser's dollar, often avail themselves of this technique. Targeted at the same market, competing publications may be making broad claims about their impact on that market. Faced with a me-too situation, a publication can (and often does) try to carve out a specific niche in which it beats out the competition. For example, several magazines claim leadership in reaching the women's market. However, one magazine distinguished itself from the others by saying that its readers use more ketchup per household than the average household of any women's service book. In other words, the publication tried to narrow its thrust so that it became a leader in some special, narrowly defined area.

This special ability can be publicized by editorializing on market research studies that demonstrate it or on case studies about ad agency media buyers who selected the publication because of it. In this way, the message can be put across not only dramatically but credibly.

PART OF SOMETHING BIGGER

Another way to avoid the problems of having a me-too product is to take a broader look at the field you are in. A company manufacturing a retail security device found itself locked in extremely tight competition with other companies marketing virtually the same product. No matter how it tried to show that its device was more reliable, its efforts might have been nullified at any moment by competition announcing a new and improved version of the product.

The problem, once again, derived from promoting the product and overlooking other promotable areas. The security device manufacturer could have avoided the problem by representing itself, instead, as an authority on retail security. Once the company has assumed that image, a lot of avenues open for it. And these are effectively pursued with PR tactics. For example, the company could hold a seminar on retail crime prevention, perhaps teleconferencing it to other participating areas of the country. (Some hotel chains offer teleconferencing facilities to link sister hotels in different areas. That way, seminar participants at one of the hotels can interact audibly and visually with those at another.) Striving for a security authority image, the security device manufacturer might have its salespeople in one locale invite prospective customers to the seminar being teleconferenced from another locale. Editors of local media, too, could be invited to attend and be handed press kits about the event (or have the kits mailed to them if they fail to show up).

By gaining exposure via publicity, the company's image as a retail security authority becomes more credible and its name more respected. And, under these circumstances, the company would certainly find it easier to compete—even with a me-too product.

Of course, a company should assume the position of an authority only if it is one. If it is as benighted about the subject as companies who are not regarded as authorities, a claim to expertise would be fraudulent, and it would introduce a new vulnerability for the company—one that competition might find impossible to ignore. On the other hand, authorities exist in every field, and they can be hired as employees or consultants. Attending teleconferenced seminars and demonstrating their knowledge of the subject, they help create the image for which the strategy was initiated.

A manufacturer of report and presentation binders found itself in the same me-too situation. In this case, the woods were filled with companies manufacturing similar binders. As a result, competition was extremely keen, and companies with the fewest promotional dollars were losing out to the big spenders. Like the security-device manufacturer, the report-binder company could sidestep its me-too product image and try to become an authority in the field. Specifically, it could become an authority on presentations. Instead of merely promoting its product, the company might sponsor and publicize seminars on how to do presentations more effectively. True, executives of the company might have to bone up on this new area or bring in outside authorities. In either case, the effort would be worth it. With its new image, the company could get a foot in the door of some of the larger companies, offering training sessions for the company's people on making effective presentations. Regarded as an authority, the company would more easily gain the confidence of prospective customers— again, in spite of its me-too product. Certainly, all the activities that could be engaged in under the banner of expertise would be grist for the publicity mill, including news releases, by-lined articles, editor interviews, and case histories. Meanwhile, all this publicity would be gaining exposure for the binder manufacturer, helping it overcome its image of a me-too company.

From the foregoing, it should be evident that there are many ways to sidestep the me-too vulnerability. Most important, a company interested in increasing its share of market (and mind) and counteracting what competition might be doing against it should seriously consider pursuing such VR strategies.

10

Changing Status

In this chapter, we will be considering the vulnerabilities a company falls heir to in such situations as plant closings, takeovers, mergers, and personnel changes—all associated with a corporate change of some kind. Such changes are generally made for the benefit of the company. Often, they are attempts to solve company problems. And, just as often, they create new—though usually less weighty—problems. Either way, a PR dilemma may result, and a PR solution must be found—especially if competition seizes the opportunity to make the most of the dilemma.

The "Plant-Closing" Vulnerability

When a large regional or national company closes down one of its stores or plants, it undoubtedly hurts employees and local tradespeople. Additionally, it gives the company's competition a chance to get the rumor mill running. It lends credence, for example, to the rumor that the company is going through hard times or failing. If the plant is responsible for producing one of the products manufactured by the company, its closing could be construed as an indication that the product is being downgraded or even discontinued. With that kind of material to work with, competition can have a field day.

Of course, in some instances, the conclusions drawn from the plant closing might be accurate. In that case, regardless of what a company does to nullify the impressions given by the closing, the effect of its PR efforts will be short-lived. In the long run, the company's various publics will realize that what they originally assumed was correct. Further, if the company, in a misguided communications program, attempts to disavow what is really happening, its credibility may be irrevocably damaged.

But when the information—possibly leaked to the public by competition—is only a rumor, then it becomes the basis for a vulnerability-relations program. It can be a multifaceted one, directed at the townspeople who would be affected by the plant closing and at other publics who do business with the company.

CONVINCING THE COMMUNITY

Let's consider a real-life example of a major company whose plant was rumored to be closing and whose product line was supposedly on the verge of being discontinued.

While company management was aware of the rumors and cognizant of their effect—which competition was wholeheartedly enjoying, if not abetting—it was unable to counteract them. Because management was unfamiliar with how public relations could be used to correct such vulnerability situations, it initially resisted the idea of using PR countermeasures. Finally, however, the PR approach seemed to be the only viable alternative—but only after it had been spelled out completely in the form of a written plan.

It is interesting to observe here how powerful the published word is, in terms of credibility. Although company management had been telling employees, customers, vendors, and townspeople that it was not considering shutting down, the claim was not believed until evidence supporting the company's position began appearing in print in the form of news.

In this instance, removing the misconception called for numerous strategic attacks on the rumor. First, paid advertising was recommended—specifically, a number of full-page ads in the local newspaper. The strategy was to demonstrate that the company was linking itself with the future of the town. The plant had been located there for 50 years, a good, round number that provided a historic milestone. Still, marking the company's fiftieth anniversary in the town was not enough to allay the townspeople's fears. To do that, the headline of the ads was designed to imply that the company was looking forward to another 50 years in town.

That was the coup de grace. It showed that the plant was not only not closing, but planning to stay on for at least as long as it had been there. Copy for the ad was meant to convince residents that the company was serious about staying. It announced a fiftieth anniversary celebration tied in with a plant open house for all the townspeople. The strategy included an invitation to employees' families to come to both the open house and a "private" plant tour, which would give the families an opportunity to see where fathers, sisters, or other relatives spent their days. Lunch, mementos, speeches, and guided tours were also planned as part of the open-house package—all carefully calculated to lend credence to the company message. The invitation list included town dignitaries and the local news media, who were to be recipients, respectively, of brochures and press kits about the company—all tied to the theme: "Looking forward to the next 50 years."

THE MARKETING APPROACH

But convincing town residents that the plant was not shutting down was winning only part of the battle. In fact, in terms of *marketing* strategy, it was the least important part. Of prime importance was convincing customers, prospects, vendors, and external sales organizations, such as reps and distributors, that the plant wasn't closing and that its product line wasn't being discontinued.

The rumor was particularly hard to disavow because it had an excellent rationale, at which competition kept hammering away. Prompting the rumor was a corporate upheaval. The company, a major U.S. manufacturer, had been merged into a still larger corporation. As a result, the company president resigned. That combination of events, coupled with what seemed to be a slow movement away from the type of product line produced by the division located in the town seemed to point to a shutdown—particularly when the idea was massaged by competition.

To undo all this on the marketing front meant directing a major program to trade and industrial publications and to the general business press. This involved reorienting the open-house press kit so that it was trade-oriented, rather than employee-oriented.

Part of the strategy included demonstrating that the open-house really had taken place. Photos were one way of documenting the event—reason, alone, for retaining a photographer for the occasion. Frequently, company executives expect attending media to provide their own photographers. Consequently, they arrange for none. This is wrong-headed, however, because the press owns whatever shots it takes and rarely makes them available to companies.

Further, the staff photographer for a particular publication may be off on another assignment and unavailable for your event —no matter how badly his editor might want it photographed. Having your own photographer present and offering his services to the media can help your company gain greater exposure in the press than you might otherwise obtain. Your photographer can ask reporters which photos or poses they'd like taken and then hand over the exposed roll of film so that the publication can develop it in its own lab. The photographer can also promise to mail the prints—if the delay is acceptable—or, in the case of a local publication, have prints messengered over the same day.

In addition to having photos of the event in the trade-oriented press kit, the documentation strategy included reproducing actual local newspaper stories about the event and incorporating them in the kit. In addition to adding further credibility, that touch provided editors with different story-treatment possibilities—which is important in maximizing exposure. The same holds true for photos. When editors receive just one photo of an event, they know that editors of other media (possibly competing ones) have the same photo to work with. So they are less inclined to use it. Since photos add to visibility of a story, it is important not to discourage editors from using the photo material you supply. Different angles and poses and photos of different scenes not only give the editor a chance to pick and choose, but increase the likelihood that other media won't be using the same shot (or not using it at all, out of fear that other media will be using it).

Also included in the press kit to the trade were executive-statement releases about the anniversary and plans for the future, as were releases talking about recent developments at the plant. All were part of the strategy to convince the company's publics that the plant was not only remaining open but also moving ahead in terms of its product lines.

Creatively, much can be done in the development of such a program. Determining how much further it is necessary to go to dispel a rumor and eliminate a vulnerability can only come from keeping an ear open to what is being said in the industry—among vendors, reps, and customers. In serious situations, benchmark studies may be in order to test if attitude changes have really occurred or if VR measures must be continued even longer.

The "Takeover" Vulnerability

When a company is either negotiating a merger or is in the early stages of undergoing one, competition can have a field day. Management of the company-to-be-merged is often blissfully unaware of the opportunities such a situation gives its competitors and may remain frozen in a do-nothing/say-nothing stance, allowing itself to be attacked at will by any company inclined to exploit its temporary advantage.

LEAKS AND RUMORS

A few years ago, a medium-sized electronics firm faced divestiture by its parent company. It was a division of a much larger organization in a totally unrelated field and had been showing bottom-line losses for a couple of years. Reasoning that it was better off sticking to its own industry, the parent company sought to divest itself of the electronics firm. That meant sounding out various potential buyers. It wasn't long before word of the intended divestiture, as well as information about the division's recent losses, leaked. Finally, one company in a similar area of the electronics field took the bait and began negotiations, which lasted several months.

To competition, those months represented a period of opportunity. Just how great an opportunity it was became evident when rumors began reaching my ears as I contacted editors about the company. One of the rumors, passed along to me by an editor, was that, because of the impending merger, the electronics company was discontinuing one of its most important product lines. It's interesting that editors—not unlike other human beings—seem to thrive on bad news. I had called the editor to pass along some good news about my client. Yet, all the editor wanted to hear was confirmation of the news that the line was being discontinued as a result of the merger plans. Since the rumor had reached the editor's ears, it was probably already circulating throughout the industry—possibly planted there or fertilized by competition. If it was, that made it even more injurious to my client in terms of its prospects for selling the product line to potential customers.

Normally, though not easily, dispelling such a rumor can be effected through various strategies—at least when the client cooperates freely. In this instance, the client, personified by the marketing vice president of the company, was unwilling to offer that cooperation. He was not sure what to say. He was stymied because he did not know what his future parent company's plans were or how management of that company might want to respond. To all intents and purposes, the vice president of marketing was paralyzed—afraid to act. Meanwhile, all sorts of rumors might have started to circulate—about products, management people, plant closings, relocations, employee layoffs, company finances, and so on.

For competition, nothing could have been more welcome. Virtually anything said about the company would have stuck for a significant amount of time—whether true or false. This gave competition an opportunity to move in and squeeze the about-to-be-merged company out of the picture. And the results of a squeeze play like that need not end after the merger. They could last forever, simply because once a competing product has been sold, say, to an end-user, the end-user has effectively been removed from the marketplace—at least until he's ready to change or upgrade his equipment.

INDIRECTNESS

So the rumor mill can have a lasting and telling effect on product sales. To prevent that from happening, countermeasures must be taken quickly. However, some responses will not work. For example, after the editor repeated to me a rumor about the product line, a simple denial by the marketing vice president would not have sufficed. To the editor and his audience, the statement would, in all likelihood, seem to have been a smokescreen, a statement contrived to mislead the reader, probably on a short-term basis—so the manufacturer could unload remaining inventory.

Probably, no direct verbal response to a rumor—say, a simple denial—can convince the audience it is intended to convince. However, this does not mean there is no way at all to confront corporate rumors. What it means is that a little creative strategy must be brought into play. In my experience, the most effective way to handle such rumors is to do it indirectly.

Accordingly, to counter the rumor that my client was discontinuing its most important product line, we made positive statements about the line. One statement was that the company had received record orders for the product, domestically and from abroad. It was issued as an executive-statement release, quoting the vice president of marketing. Obviously, the line was not about to be dropped if it was getting record sales, which in turn would lead to add-on sales among the original purchasers (as is normal with the kind of equipment involved).

Another executive-statement release pointed out that the company had just completed an expansion and modernization of its production facilities for the product line.

It is important to emphasize that the rumored merger was never denied—directly or indirectly. Because the merger was a possibility, any kind of refutation might have destroyed the company's credibility for quite some time.

It is also important to note that, although company executives were unable to say anything definite about the future of the product line and its continuance—largely because they were ignorant of the plans of their would-be parent company—they had no trouble issuing the kinds of statements they did. The company *had* racked up record sales in the product line and it *had* just completed a facility expansion and modernization for the line.

The idea, then, is to find some areas about which positive statements can be made—statements that indirectly deny the rumor.

The product itself can provide ammunition to counter such a rumor. In this instance, we interested editors in interviewing the director of engineering about enhancements he was planning for the product line. If the line was being discontinued, the enhancements would not be in the offing. A continuous flow of product publicity was planned for the product—by similar editor interviews and product releases. The exposure that resulted during the merger period helped stifle the rumor that the line was being phased out.

The positive-statement approach used in counteracting one kind of vulnerability can similarly be used in other vulnerability situations, which we'll see as we proceed. The important lesson in the case of mergers or takeovers is not to allow company executives to be frozen into a no-response position. That is precisely what competition is counting on, allowing it to make whatever statements about the company it wants, knowing the statements will go unchallenged. By finding noncorporate ways of countering the rumor (e.g., factual product and sales statements, instead of statements about the direction the business will be taking), you can beat competition at its own game.

The "Personnel" Vulnerability

Although people are the stuff companies are made of, most vulnerabilities have to do with "things" instead. Nevertheless, as we'll demonstrate here, people—management and other employees—can also be the source of a company's VR problem.

In one such instance, an electronics manufacturing company had recently changed hands. Some time after the arrival of the new management, my PR organization came on the scene. During the course of conducting my usual audit, I found that the company's previous management had been involved in practices that were not in the best traditions of the business world. Because the company was not a large one, news of the management shift was not on everyone's lips. In fact, few in the industry and few existing and potential customers knew anything about the changeover.

This general lack of knowledge proved to be harmful to the company. The business practices of the previous management, if not already known by *potential* customers, were certainly known by competition. And the negative information was probably not kept secret. Thus, although a new and quite different management had taken over—one that was earnest, hard-working, and committed to producing the best possible product and service for customers—the company retained its bad reputation.

As a result, the company found itself in difficulty on several fronts. It found it hard to maintain a top-flight rep organization because better-quality reps didn't want to tarnish their images by representing the company. In addition, previous management had not been feeding sales leads to the reps, as initially promised. Further, potential customers shied away from buying products from the company because of the reputation of previous management. Suppliers, too, were not eager to sell to the company because of questionable payment practices. (It seems it is much easier for a bad reputation to spread than for a good one to take its place.)

All in all, the new management was in trouble. Even the salespeople, customers, and suppliers who knew about the change found it hard to believe that the new regime wasn't merely a surrogate for the previous one, which was lurking in the shadows someplace, still calling the shots.

AN UPHILL CLIMB

The PR assignment was to restore the credibility of the company so that the world-at-large realized that there was, indeed, new management of the highest caliber. One of the ways we attempted to do this was by establishing confidence in the new management. This was achieved in part by positioning present management executives as industry authorities. That was no fabrication, because the executives were considerably knowledgeable in their field. Once given the opportunity to appear as authorities, we reasoned, they would be able to hold their own.

The attempt to gain exposure for the new management involved PR *and* advertising. The PR approach was threefold. First, we authored a series of semitechnical articles (readable both by engineers and by management) under the marketing vice president's by-line and placed them with numerous leading industrial publications. Well-researched, they offered the reader extremely valuable information on purchasing, screening, installing, and trouble-shooting electronic products of this type. The articles were well received (one garnered an award from the publisher) and were reprinted several times to fulfill the demand by companies for additional copies.

Next, we developed a series of editorial-looking ads bearing the vice president's by-line and a catchy title that was repeated, ad after ad, at the very top. It impressed readers as a regularly-appearing guest-editor's column discussing the product category. The ads were scheduled to appear in only a few of the top publications in the client's market. (Too many publications would have spread the limited ad budget too thin.) We decided to use a series of editorial-looking *ads* instead of actual editorial matter—which might be considered the normal PR approach—in order to guarantee that the audiences for those particular publications would be reached again and again by the company's executive in the role of an authority advising them about the product. By itself, PR might not have been able to appear in the same form as regularly as would a scheduled ad that resembled an editorial column.

In addition to the articles and editorial-column ads, executive-statement news releases were submitted to the media, with leadership-type observations by the vice president about industry problems. Also, industry seminars were arranged so that the vice president would be able to gain exposure as an authority before live audiences—and get written up for what he said in the trade press.

One major objective was to restore credibility in the firm by establishing the credibility of its management. Eventually, we included several executives in the program. Initially, however, we focused on just one—the man who probably would have more opportunities for public exposure (e.g., at trade shows) than other executives of the company. To increase his recognizability, we accompanied our executive-statement releases, by-lined feature articles, roundup article quotes, and the by-lined ad with a head-and-shoulders photo of him. The strategy worked. When accompanying reps on visits to prospects or attending trade shows, he was easily identified as the authority whose articles or statements potential customers had read. While a negative image doesn't change overnight, this approach did much to alter the image established by previous management.

LOSING AN EXECUTIVE

Management turnover in itself is a form of vulnerability that competition can use to its advantage. It may be rumored, for example, that a high-level executive is leaving and taking along some major accounts. Repeated in the right places, this rumor can raise fears in the minds of prospective or existing customers that the company may be weakened or go under as a result of the account losses.

If the rumor is wrong and the executive has no intention of leaving the company, straight-out denials will do little to stifle it. A false rumor must be handled indirectly, which can be done in various ways. The executive might be made the center of a story about the company; he might give talks whenever possible about his faith in the future of the company; or he might be on the receiving end of some honor bestowed on him by the company— all of which could be given PR treatment. The resulting exposure would tend to demonstrate indirectly that these things just wouldn't be happening if the executive harbored any thoughts about leaving the company.

Of course, if the rumor about the executive's departure happens to be true, then it must not be denied. What little relief such an untruth would offer the company would, at best, be short-lived. At the same time, it would destroy the credibility of future company statements.

In some instances, the loss of an executive—rumored or not— may lead to other than account-loss fears. For example, it may harbinger a change in management philosophy. In that case, competition might find opportunities to show that, as a result of the loss, the company will revert to "the old ways"—which might have been old-fashioned or contrary to the interests of various of the company's publics (e.g., shareholders, reps, distributors, customers, and suppliers).

AN ORGANIZATIONAL PROBLEM

It should be getting clearer and clearer that virtually everything that occurs with respect to a company must be studied from the point of view of how competition might utilize it for strategic gain. It should also be obvious that direct responses to those situations don't work. As we've seen, PR techniques provide a way to respond to vulnerability situations by making an "end run" around them. That way, the company doesn't appear to be worried and trying to hide the truth. If R&D, for example, were losing personnel, an indirect response indicating that R&D was being expanded or improved would dispel any negative thoughts about the company that the outside world might be harboring.

A major corporation found that the way its personnel were assigned one-product-only responsibilities in the sales area was providing a vulnerability that competition was using to great advantage. The solution was to alter the salespeople's activities so that each person was responsible for the company's full line of products. That restructuring, which was highly publicized, erased any suggestions initiated by competition that customers of the corporation had to deal with an army of people if they wanted to buy different products or if something was wrong with different pieces of equipment. With the new structure, that was no longer necessary. One person was able to handle anything that the customer needed. That company had what might be designated "organization-chart" vulnerability. The problem was not covered up, which might have left the company open to criticism by its competition. Instead, the problem was communicated to the public quite openly —along with a full account of the solution.

A MOVING STRATEGY

In another case, a long-established engineering company seemed on the verge of losing its middle management executives and key engineers as the result of a move to another state. This provided competition with plenty of opportunities to spread the word. Rumors were flying that the company was going under, had to cut expenses and, as a result, was losing a major part of its top-echelon team. In reality, the move was not a cost-cutting effort. Instead, it was costing the company a great deal of money. The company was moving in order to have company management close to the pilot plant—a vital part of the engineering operation— making the company more efficient and offering customers better service.

The problem was that many top people did not want to uproot themselves and make the move. The best approach to this vulnerability was to say nothing to the public until an attempt had been made by the company to change things for the better. Denying that their top people were not relocating to the new headquarters would eventually have been found to be false. Instead, a major employee-centered program was launched. Its goal was to convince executives who didn't want to relocate that their fears of moving were not justified. A major element of the program was getting town officials and realtors from the new headquarters site to put on a presentation to the employees about the new area. Fortunately, the officials and realtors agreed to visit the company and uncorked an appealing presentation about the new community—its religious, school, and entertainment facilities; hospitals and shopping centers; homebuying and apartment rental costs; costs of living in the area compared with costs back home; transportation (e.g., buses, trains, airlines); and costs of visiting friends and relatives left behind.

In addition, the company subscribed to local newspapers and had them delivered for several months preceding the move to the homes of company employees. This enabled them to read the food ads to compare prices, to peruse the classified ads to locate houses and apartments, and to see what jobs were available for others in their immediate families. All moving expenses, plus legal assistance in terminating existing leases and responsibility for the sale of existing homes, were assumed by the company.

When all was said and done, more than three-quarters of the company's key people moved to the new headquarters location. Most of them were people who initially had stated that they wouldn't be relocating and had intended to leave the company.

Now the story was tellable. Releases were issued describing the company's move to new headquarters and profiling its key people who were moving with it. In addition, facets of the employee relations program were told via releases, articles, and interviews with editors, dramatizing in numerous ways that the company was not losing its employees, nor were they leaving because the company was on the skids. These various PR approaches also provided an indirect way for the company to deny what competition was saying and to tell the inside story on the moving of its headquarters: To better serve its customers, the company was really spending heavily on the move—not tightening its belt because of hard times.

The timing of public announcements about the move was crucial to the overall strategy. Had announcements been made too soon, competition might have jumped on them as so much propaganda. By the time the announcements were actually made, how-

ever, there was no longer a possibility that they could be inter-
preted as a smokescreen for a company that, in reality, was going
downhill.

AN ANTI-SEXIST STRATEGY

In still another instance of "personnel" vulnerability, a security guard company was being maligned because of its employee
hiring policy. In this case, the attack was sexist. Competitive
guard companies tried to show that the company's practice of hiring female security guards was not in the best interests of its clients. Of course, there was no way to deny that female guards were
being employed. They were. And they were doing a good job. The
way to handle such a vulnerability, we felt, was to present the
female guards as positively (and as truthfully) as possible. We had
studies done of comparable situations in which female and male
guards were used and then compared how effectively each handled
the situations. In many instances, female guards handled them
better. What the studies showed was that sometimes women
guards were better, sometimes male guards were better, and sometimes gender made no difference at all.

Then we published these findings, as well as case histories
involving female guards, showing them off in situations where
they performed extremely well. Where crowds and near-panic
situations were involved, it was shown that female guards were
able to restore calm and help people regain control of their emo-
tions more effectively. Female guards also tended to make males,
who might otherwise have acted unruly, behave in a more reasonable, more gallant manner. Quite often, it turned out, the presence
of a female guard was more reassuring to certain types of people.
All these instances provided excellent material to publicize in local
and national media. Again, there was no attempt to hide the fact
that the security firm was employing female guards. Instead, the
practice was presented to the media and to the public as reasonable
and practical. In fact, it allowed the security firm to provide better
service than its competitors who chided it for hiring female
guards. Once again, a vulnerability was turned into an asset by
careful presentation of the facts in a nonpropagandistic way—using PR strategies.

11

Losing Face

As we've seen, competition appears to maintain a constant vigil, ever watchful for some chink in your armor that will give it a competitive advantage. These chinks may or may not exist. When they do, expect your competitor's salespeople to charge right in and make the most of them. When they don't exist, don't put it past your competitor to imply that they do.

Let's look now at some chinks that may result from the slipshod practices of a company—habits or practices that a company may let itself slip into that tend to tarnish its image.

The "Tardy-Delivery" Vulnerability

At one time or another, many companies inadvertently gain a reputation for slow deliveries. Whether it is deliveries of merchandise to a distributor or a retailer or delivery of heavy equipment to an industrial end-user, it has the same effect. The customer would rather try his luck with a source that has a better reputation for promptness.

A reputation for tardiness cannot be treated lightly. A company might very well be waiting to incorporate your product line into one of its own—say, a radio manufacturer in need of your dials or printed circuits. Or it might be a retailer eager to tie in with a sudden peak in consumer demand and afraid of getting stuck with merchandise delivered after the demand has already peaked and is on the wane.

In these and similar situations, being known as a company that doesn't deliver on time can be deadly. At the very least, it's a vulnerability—whether it's true or it's just a rumor contrived by your competition. As such, it must be tackled with the same purposeful attitude you would assume with other types of vulnerabilities.

Suppose your company has developed a reputation for not delivering its product on time and that, as rumor has it, the fault lies with an outmoded inventory control and parts warehousing system. Examining a problem like this can be an excellent exercise in developing strategies to cope with this and other types of vulnerability.

BEING SPECIFIC

Essentially, the objective is to undo this late-delivery image. It doesn't help to show what an excellent product you have. Nobody cares—if it arrives after your customer needs it. And no amount of advertising about the quality of your product will change the image. Nor will evidence of the company's stability, its fine R&D facilities, or its long-term warrantee.

The point is that *specific* vulnerabilities do their damage in *specific* ways. And the damage must be undone in equally specific ways. No amount of promotional expenditure covering other features of the product or company can be fully successful until that specific vulnerability is at least neutralized and, if possible, turned into a positive asset.

How can late deliveries be turned into a positive asset? The answer is not in speeding up deliveries. Certainly, that's important. But it can only come as an adjunct to the right strategy. Correcting the vulnerability—if it exists—just isn't enough. Documentation of that correction is what's needed, so that *total* markets become aware of it—not just those who are receiving deliveries. Moreover, in order to be credible, the documentation must be effected by a third party—not by a member of the vulnerable company. That third party is the news media that reaches the markets in question.

Here are a few ways of gaining news media exposure to counteract the late-delivery image. A little thought on the subject should generate all sorts of approaches—just one approach usually isn't enough to undo the harm a vulnerability can do to a company.

It is important to stress one point before we review examples of possible VR strategies: *Truthfulness is essential.* A company can't lie about cleaning up a slow delivery problem when it hasn't. Competition can quickly determine whether you have taken corrective measures, as you are claiming. And a lie, on top of the already-established vulnerability, can become a powerful weapon in your competitor's hands.

BEING CREATIVE

Assume that your company has corrected the problem (if the problem really existed)—for example, by instituting a new system in its inventory control procedures and in its shipping department. The next step is to let the affected markets and prospective customers know about it. That can be done through one or more executive-statement releases targeted at news editors of publications serving the markets. The statements might mention new personnel appointments in the problem areas—possibly high-level people brought in to correct the deficiency. Other releases might mention new equipment moved into those areas. And still others might discuss a new system being used to expedite orders. Directed at the news columns of industry publications, these releases will be read by your customers and other publics, and—because they are editorial in nature—they will have a high degree of credibility.

One creative approach might be to convince the editor of a publication in the materials-handling field, for example, that your company has instituted a new system that his readers would be interested in learning about so they can emulate it. If you are lucky, the editor might discuss the new system in a feature article written by his staff. Or he might ask your company to prepare an article—possibly with photos to illustrate it. Once the article appears in print, it can be reprinted and used as a handout or a mailer to prospective and existing customers. This tactic would, indeed, get across the fact that you've adopted the new system and that it is a valuable problem-solver for your company—so much so, in fact, that a publication in the materials-handling field thought it worthy of feature coverage.

This brings up another important issue that we've touched on previously: It isn't always necessary for the editorial exposure you get to appear in the media serving the market your company is trying to influence. As in the example just cited, the materials-handling publication might never have been read by your prospects or customers. But merchandising the article through reprints gives it rifle-shot impact at your target markets and gets across the third-party support that is vital for credibility.

It might even be possible to convince a publication or organization to present your company with some sort of award for the new system you've installed. That would surely be newsworthy and could be the basis for a series of executive-statement releases, news-item coverage in a variety of media targeted at the company's markets, and even some highly convincing feature articles describing the system and possibly alluding to the previous problems your company had been having with meeting delivery dates.

There is nothing wrong, by the way, with acknowledging that a problem existed. It can, in fact, be very powerful in convincing the outside world that you really are a truthful organization and that you are prepared to accept responsibility for past inadequacies. Prospects or customers are apt to think more highly of companies that own up to problems they've had. Overcoming such problems is admirable and, in a way, heroic. Of course, some companies absolutely refuse to confess to either a past problem or one that is being corrected, even though all of its customers are aware of the problem. However, that attitude only makes life more difficult for a company's sales and marketing people, who must, in face-to-face encounters, deny what everyone is talking about. That in itself casts doubt on a company's truthfulness and gives rise to still another kind of vulnerability that is one's own doing (and can be one's undoing).

Again, finding ways to counter vulnerabilities is very much a matter of creativity. You zero in on the specific type of vulnerability your company has and then let your imagination get to work. There's no telling how many strategic approaches you're apt to come up with.

The "Fuddy-Duddy" Vulnerability

No company can escape exhibiting some form of vulnerability. And whatever it is, competition may try to benefit by it—even if it doesn't really exist. We have seen how a new company or one entering a new market has a newcomer vulnerability. Getting older doesn't help matters, either. At some point, any company can acquire the "fuddy-duddy" vulnerability, which is just as bad. A company could be doing something the same way year after year —a way that has proved to be efficient, advantageous, and economical. Yet, competition stands ready to point an accusing finger, intimating to prospective customers that the company is behind the times—either in its marketing, its product development, its manufacturing, or its methods of doing business. The implication might be that the product is unimproved, manufacturing or R&D equipment is outdated, processing methods are old, or even quality controls instituted by the company are not up to current standards.

Needless to say, such innuendos can do a lot to hurt a company's prospects in the marketplace, whether its product is aimed at businesses or consumers. As a result, retailers may be wary of inventorying a product that takes up valuable shelf space, while newer products gain consumer preference and sales. Industrial organizations would no doubt shy away from outdated products, too, whether the products are used for plant maintenance or used as a component of their own product, as in the case of an OEM. Such "outdated" products can find a market only if their manufacturer offers enticing price concessions—definitely a disadvantage if the manufacturer is interested (as he should be) in growth and increased share of market.

As always in a vulnerability situation, the company must first determine whether the vulnerability is real. If it is, then something must be done to correct it. Only after it has been corrected should communications strategies be initiated to counter the negative image.

When the vulnerability is fictitious, then VR procedures ought to be set in motion immediately.

AN ORGANIZATIONAL APPROACH

One major company subject to this type of competitive offensive was in a high-technology industry. It discovered that it was acquiring the image of a laggard, both in new technology development and new product introductions. Such an image hurts a company not only in the marketplace, but also—if the company is a public one—on Wall Street. Who would want to invest in the securities of a firm with such an image? A privately held company seeking additional funding through private channels could also be damaged by such an image.

In this case, intent on overcoming its negative image, the company began publicizing the positive aspects of its internal organization. One of these was a new-development department formed expressly to investigate current existing technology, evaluate its potential, and develop it into a product.

One publicity approach was to interest editors in feature articles on how a new-development department works and how such a department might help others, just as it had helped this company. The idea was to show that the company was avant garde in its methods and could therefore set an example for other companies.

Another publicity approach was to form a department that consisted of a group of some of its senior, most experienced people. The mission for this group was to seek out new avenues for the company to explore. It was cut loose from all other responsibilities and given totally free rein to explore new ideas. Like the new-development department, the "brain trust" was extremely publicizable. Even the establishment of the group merited news releases. Senior executives of the company could issue comments via executive-statement releases on the advantages of the group not only to the company, but to the industry and to the entire business community. In addition, members of the group could be interviewed individually by consumer and trade media. And feature articles about the operation of the group, as well as how other companies could follow suit, could be drafted and placed with appropriate media. The throw-off from such a barrage of material on this subject would maximize exposure opportunities for the company—all directing attention to the fact that the company is not a fuddy-duddy, but is looking long and hard at the future.

THE BENEFITS OF TELLING ALL

If the vulnerabilities actually exist, there are constructive ways to communicate to the company's publics that things have changed—or are changing. One well-known distributor decided that it should own up to its previous shortcomings. "Confessing," it seems, holds a certain fascination for the media. The distributor, who was clever enough to realize that fact, turned his confession into an editor attention-getter and gained lots of exposure for the company's positively oriented story.

In fact, the distributor accomplished a VR coup of sorts by seizing the opportunity to get the jump on his competition. He did this by showing, via major business publication exposure, how he had upgraded the methods by which he does things. This upgrading might never have warranted the media exposure it received had it not been linked with a confession from the company. This was definitely a creative approach, carefully calculated to capitalize on a fondness common to many editors for this particular type of story.

Confessing also appeals to the public's attitude toward an underdog. In the case of the distributor, potential customers who saw the story were sympathetic toward the company—particularly because it overcame its shortcomings and pioneered methods more advanced than those of other distributors.

INSTITUTIONS DO IT, TOO

We hardly ever suspect that museums compete with one another. They do, however, when they go after funding or new collections. A real fuddy-duddy vulnerability situation came to light in this field when one museum intimated that a competing museum was stodgy in its methods and inappropriate for receiving certain grants and collections that it sought for itself. Meanwhile, the so-called stodgy museum, in the best tradition of vulnerability relations, launched a media-information program that catapulted it into the spotlight as a museum deeply involved with research and analysis of new developments in the field. This was accomplished by issuing a steady stream of news releases to the media critiquing developments of interest to collectors and others interested in the history, art, and craftsmanship connected with museum collections. Thus, a seemingly placid institution bared its knuckles to engage in what could have been a struggle for the museum's very survival. What is most interesting here is that we commonly think of marketing tactics in connection with products or services, but rarely with institutions. This is an example of how an organization with a small budget can gain meaningful exposure through the media.

As an extension of the museum's publicity program, guest

shots for its curators might have been arranged on TV talk shows. And seminars might have been held on new developments in particular fields of interest to collectors. Also, articles might have been written on controversial topics connected with certain collectibles.

Getting involved in controversy, as a matter of fact, is an excellent way to gain exposure. It can position the person making the statement—be it pro or con—as an authority. It also tends to get better-than-average coverage and better position in the media. It is well worth the PR practitioner's time to seek out controversial issues involving his company's or client's industry and have company executives make statements about them.

A word about getting onto talk shows. They are not only important vehicles for exposure, but also in great abundance on radio and TV. Virtually every local station schedules them— sometimes covering national topics and sometimes focusing on topics of import to local, industrial, medical, scientific, religious, farm, and sports interests. Just about any type of company can get exposure opportunities on talk shows that in some way relate to what it does. Exposure needn't end there, either. Knowing of such guest shots in advance, the PR staff can get prepublicity out to the media—trade or consumer—about them. At the show itself, a photo of the participating company executive might be taken. Captioned or accompanied by a news release, it would provide another opportunity for media pick-up. Also during the show, a video or audio taping might be done. Duplicates of these tapes could be produced for use in presentations and at trade shows. Then, following the show, a release could be distributed to the media on the guest appearance of the company executive and on what transpired on the show. PR treatment before, during, and after thus offers important opportunities for exposure. Events should always be examined for this triple-punch approach.

VARIOUS APPROACHES

An opening event of some sort is an excellent vehicle for demonstrating that new things are happening. It might be the opening of a new plant, warehouse, or office; the inauguration of a new service; the availability of new facilities; or the introduction of a new product line. In many cases, these opening events can be treated with considerable fanfare—speeches, invited dignitaries, catered food, press kits, tours for customers and the media, etc. Particularly important is seeking opportunities to use such tactics when a fuddy-duddy vulnerability is known to exist. They demonstrate visibly that the company is on the move, that things are happening and, in spite of what people may be saying to the contrary, that the company is in no way stagnating or resting on its laurels.

Companies also miss lots of opportunities for creating an on-the-move impression. They do it by overlooking little changes or improvements that can be dramatized through PR. Even a new machine that will be installed in the plant can be photographed as it is being brought into the building. The photo can then be sent to the media with a caption or release about the new equipment and its role in improving production. Information about such matters should somehow reach the ears of the PR staff, which can evaluate it for exposure opportunities. That's just one more reason for PR people to be intimately involved with company changes and to be brought in at every opportunity—and not just sporadically for projects that company executives consider important.

The "All-Eggs-in-One-Basket" Vulnerability

Research reports indicate that many companies do a large percentage of their business with a small percentage of customers. The figures vary somewhat. But, by and large, they show that many companies rely on a tiny customer base.

Of course, companies are always trying to broaden their market. But try as they might, it seems that most of their sales remain with only a small portion of their potential customers. Although it is a more or less normal condition, competition can turn it into a serious vulnerability.

Consider the consequences of doing the bulk of your business with only a few customers. It's nice to boast about various Fortune 500 companies as major accounts. But what happens if you should lose them?

That possibility doesn't begin and end as an internal problem that concerns only your company. It has tentacles that extend to the outside world—to shareholders, private investors, suppliers, and customers.

Shareholders would certainly be interested in whether you lost a major account. It would affect company income and the return on their investment—possibly through lowering the price of the stock or the dollar value of the dividend. Realizing the risk a company runs by having its most valuable eggs in a few baskets, the shareholders may think twice before investing in the company.

Private investors will evaluate a company by the same standards. Would they be jeopardizing their money by investing in such a company?

And what of the supplier? What does he have to lose? It is not too evident that he is affected at all. Yet, he is. He may be extending large amounts of credit to the company, while shipping it vast quantities of merchandise. What happens if it loses a major account? Is there a possibility that the company might be unable to honor its debt—possibly paying the vendor only a few cents on the dollar, if at all? Clearly, the vendor might be scared off in such a situation. And he scares off prospective customers who realize that the company may have difficulty locating another vendor to sell it the merchandise it needs. Further, the prospective customer certainly considers the financial stability of a firm with which it places a large (and possibly continuing) order. When that financial stability may be threatened, the customer may opt to do business with a competitor.

SIMPLE COUNTER-STRATEGIES

This situation, incidentally, is not unlike one we covered earlier. A company that has an all-eggs-in-one-basket vulnerability may nevertheless point its finger accusingly at another company in the same situation, which is easy to do since many companies are in that situation. The "exposed" company finds itself an underdog even though it never regarded its situation as a vulnerability.

Like other types of vulnerability, there are ways a company can diminish the impact of this type. Obviously, the counteraction must demonstrate that the company has, in reality, spread its risk over a broad customer base.

Such counter-activity is most credibly done through PR, using VR strategies. They needn't be very complicated strategies. For example, the company could institute a program in which the opening of new accounts is publicly announced through press releases to the various media. Such announcements appear frequently in trade publications, as well as in *The Wall Street Journal* (in the case of major contracts for public corporations) and *The New York Times*. Generally, these releases get little space—usually, no more than a line or two. Nevertheless, these brief notices are well read since the publication's readers often turn specifically to the relevant section or column to learn about current business activity.

It is possible, however, to obtain a greater amount of space—particularly in trade publications—by accompanying the release with a photograph. Let's suppose that a customer has decided to buy a new machine from your company. He'll probably sign an agreement and, after it's signed, shake hands with your sales representative. Well, those two acts—signing and shaking hands—may be corny, but they recur constantly in the pages of trade magazines. The photo accompanying the release could show either the signing or the handshake. Properly captioned and mailed together with the news release about the new sale or contract, the photo encourages the editor to grant your story more space and gives it a greater chance of attracting the reader's attention. It's even possible to have a photo taken some time after the actual signing. The salesman may be on the road and unable to get back to the customer for quite a while. But when he does, it's a good idea to have a local photographer standing by to take the shot. Then the original signing or handshaking can be replayed for the benefit of the photographer.

It isn't very difficult to arrange to have a local photographer at the site, even if it is thousands of miles away from your office. One way is to call the local newspaper and speak with the photo editor. He may refer you to the paper's own photographer who does moonlighting, or he may put you in touch with a local photographer he knows. There are also commercial organizations (usually in large cities) that specialize in acting as middlemen to get you a photographer, no matter where the photo site may be. Usually, such an arrangement costs more than if the photographer worked directly for you. But this way, it's a lot easier. And usually the middlemen know who the good photographers are. Either route is far less expensive than paying a photographer from your town to travel to the contract-signing location.

Another easily administered program designed to demonstrate a high-activity level in the opening of accounts is the presentation of awards, with subsequent publicizing of the presentation. How does this get across the idea of intense new account activity? Consider giving awards to salespeople who do particularly well in the account-opening department. It could be a periodic event—even monthly—so that a steady stream of new-account news is ready for release to the media, month after month.

In addition, you can announce that the company has achieved a milestone—and add a ceremony to dramatize it. The milestone could be the thousandth customer, or any appropriate number. Publicizing the event with releases, a dinner, speeches, awards, and statements about company goals and achievements can go a long way toward demonstrating to the public that the company's account base is far from small.

THE SUPPLIER SYNDROME

One particular all-eggs-in-one-basket vulnerability is harder to notice. Yet, it might blossom, nurtured by a competitor, into a full-blown argument against doing business with your company. This one has to do with suppliers. It might even be called the "supplier-weak-link" vulnerability. It can involve the supplier of an almost insignificant item, yet one on which the manufacture of your product depends. For example, it might be something as trivial as a button, without which many a suit of clothes would remain incomplete and left on the hanger.

This vulnerability may arise because your sole supplier of a particular item is going on strike. What then are customers who are waiting for your finished product going to do until the strike is settled? Very likely, they will turn in desperation to your competitor, who will be waiting in the wings, only too happy to step in and take on the additional business.

In such a situation, it is important that the affected company demonstrate that other sources of supply are available. Again, this could be done by an award. But this time, it might be your supplier who awards you for being a valued (or largest, or oldest, or one-thousandth) customer. Don't wait until your supplier thinks of giving your company an award or feels you deserve it. Suggest it yourself and even work with the supplier to prepare the award and plan the presentation.

It might even be possible to author an article or grant an editor interview on the benefits of having more than one source of supply. While such an article may ostensibly be tutorial, it has the hidden strategy of revealing to prospective customers that you have not placed all your eggs in the basket of a single supplier.

OTHER SITUATIONS

These strategies should be effective in a variety of supplier-related situations. For example, it could suddenly come to light that one of your suppliers has a poor quality-control program. Dramatizing that your company depends on several suppliers and not just one would placate customers who fear that your production will be hindered as a result or that you will be forced to employ poor-quality components in your product—just to be able to continue production and delivery.

The point is that vulnerabilities are contagious. They are relayed from company to company, backwards and forwards along the path of distribution. Thus, if one of your main suppliers is in financial difficulty, you may be wary of doing business with him. However, until you do something about it, his vulnerability is *your* vulnerability, because your customers, knowing of your dependence on the supplier, may suddenly become wary of *your* company. Faced with a potentially vulnerable supplier, it is good judgment for you to include some countermeasures in your regular public relations program, just as a matter of self-protection.

An unusual type of all-eggs-in-one-basket vulnerability involving a company and its labor union recently came to light. Suspecting that it might become vulnerable because of a strike at one of its plants, the company publicized that it was strike-proof. It was, indeed, because each of its plants was represented by a different union. This was a powerful way to fight back against competitors who produced similar products. That a competitor might be represented by a single union is a fact that a smaller, multiunion company could use to its advantage. Should a strike be called against the competitor, its customers would lose a major source of supply. The knowledge that another company in the field would be able to continue deliveries in the face of a strike would be a strong inducement to give it business.

The all-eggs-in-one-basket vulnerability is a multifaceted one that can at times be used as an awesome weapon by competition. It is useful to consider *all* the situations in which this vulnerability might exist and to institute a program that either eliminates or at least diminishes its impact. How intensive a VR program should be depends, of course, on the likelihood that competition will use the vulnerability to its advantage.

The "No-Demand" Vulnerability

Still another vulnerability has to do with demand for your product or service. One of the few unalterable laws of economics is the demand/price ratio. If demand for a product or service increases, the price can be raised. If demand drops—either because the price is too high or interest in the product or service has waned—the price must be lowered until it reaches a point at which demand again increases. Dropping the price too low might result in a financial loss for the seller. At some point, he might have to discontinue the product or service.

Of course, nothing would please your competitors more than seeing you drop out of the market—other than seeing you fail to enter it in the first place. And regardless of the real or potential demand for your product, competition can help bring about either result by spreading the news that nobody is really interested in the product—that there is little or no demand for it.

COMPETITORS RISE TO THE OCCASION

This no-demand strategy can be used for all types of products —customer, commercial, technical, or industrial. It can be used to influence retailers, sales reps, wholesalers, and distributors. It matters little whether the company marketing the product is large or small.

In one instance, a very large company in the photo-equipment business found that competition was beginning to threaten its markets. A major company in the same industry had begun to produce a very similar piece of equipment.

Cleverly, the threatened company decided that key elements

in the design of its product could be applied effectively to other industries. The decision to enter these markets promised to provide the company with a source of revenue beyond the reach of its aggressive competitor. So the company began manufacturing and marketing these innovative products in fields it had never set foot in before. The outstanding name it had developed in its principal field, management felt, would help it get a toe-hold in the new industries.

However, breaking into new markets was not as easy as it seemed. While competitors in the company's original field were unconcerned about the innovative products for other fields, companies already in those fields were quite concerned. More than that, they tried to set up roadblocks that would prevent or delay inroads into their markets.

In part, the roadblocks consisted of downplaying the value of these innovations in their fields. The established companies claimed that the products were too advanced for the needs of their markets. They also contended that the products were as yet untried. Why bother with imponderables, they said, when old standbys—which could be depended on to operate successfully and to last a reasonable amount of time—were available? This counterstrategy by the photo-equipment company's new-found competition came as a surprise. Because the products the company was offering were so unique, management felt that competition would be minimal. Yet competitors, hoping to protect their markets against this new intruder, criticized the uniqueness as an unnecessary novelty.

These manufacturers, who had long been entrenched in the new markets, also labeled the photo-equipment company a parvenu. They argued that the company, though well known, was nevertheless a newcomer to those industries, possibly only venturing from its own field for a short time as a "rescue" effort, while it was trying to solve its problems in the photo-equipment field. In that case, why buy from a company that might pull out and stop doing business in these new fields when things got better in its own?

The newcomer tag, as we've seen, is calculated to persuade potential buyers to reject the newcomer in favor of companies who, as old-timers in the industry, are not about to pack up suddenly and disappear. Established customers can be told that if they switch to the newcomer and he picks up stakes and moves out, there may be no suppliers left, and customers would be left high and dry.

The no-demand ploy can also be used by competition when the target company is definitely no newcomer to the field or commitment to that particular industry doesn't even enter the picture. When safety bindings for skis were first introduced, entrenched binding manufacturers tried to protect themselves and their traditional binding designs by arguing that no skier would want a binding that might release from his foot at any time, endangering him even more than the no-release type.

When the automated-exposure camera was first introduced, competition again implied there would be no demand for it. Who would want a camera that limited artistic expression by taking shutter speed out of the control of the photographer?

Of course, both the safety binding for skis and the automated camera have become firmly established products. Nevertheless, competitors of the original manufacturers of these innovative products had no qualms about raising doubts in the retailers' and consumers' minds about the practicality of such equipment and didn't hesitate to predict a lack of demand for them.

Such arguments can be used effectively by competitors to dissuade manufacturers, retailers, distributors, and sales reps from buying or taking on a new product. For a manufacturer, the argument might be that the product is unnecessarily innovative, that it hasn't proven itself, or that the company making it might pull out, leaving no second source of supply. For a retailer, the argument might be that the product has little or no demand for it—possibly because of its high price, its newness, or its manufacturer's lack of experience in the field.

The no-demand argument carries a lot of weight with end-users, as well as with resellers. Companies like to know that others are using the product—and using it successfully. If no one is buying, it's better to stick with the tried and true.

Price and equality can also be used in the no-demand strategy launched by competition. If price is high because the product is complex or innovative, competition can use this to convince retailers, distributors, and others that nobody wants the product. The same argument can be used against quality. Who needs a product that can last forever, for example, when good, serviceable merchandise is available elsewhere at a lower price? High quality isn't always a good selling point, and in the hands of a skilled competitor, it can be turned into a deterrent against buying the product.

DOCUMENTING DEMAND

Faced with this type of no-demand situation—whether inspired by competition or not—what can a company do to overcome it? Let's examine a few vulnerability-relations techniques and see how they might influence matters.

As we've just seen, companies like to know that the product they purchase has been used successfully by others, whether in or out of their own industry. Naturally, a salesperson can try to prove that the product has been widely accepted by making the rounds of prospective end-users and telling them which companies are using his company's equipment. But that is a slow, tedious way of letting a lot of end-users everywhere know about a product. Sales calls are expensive; they must be done one at a time; and they lack a certain degree of credibility because the salesperson would never say anything bad about his own company's product. And even if he asked the prospect to call up or visit end-users for proof of how pleased they are with the product, the visits might not breed confidence. They might be a set-up. The end-user companies might be particularly friendly toward the salesperson or his company, or they might be the only companies that have had good results with the product.

On the other hand, reading an article about an end-user who purchased the product—and is happy he did—has a lot more credibility, as far as the prospect is concerned. That's because the magazine editor is inserted between the company and the end-user testimonial. That solitary fact makes all the difference. It brings to the situation the stature that the editor has built up over a period of time or that the magazine has established with its readers. Now, when the end-user says he's pleased with the product, the prospect who has seen the article really believes that there is a legitimate demand for it.

Another alternative might be a testimonial-type advertisement about the end-user's satisfaction with the product. But an advertisement is no substitute for an article. It, too, might be a set-up, based on a friendship between the end-user and the manufacturer. Or the end-user might be one of the few buyers who has used the product successfully.

The type of article that should be used for this purpose is the case-history feature. Reduced to its barest essentials, it states the problems the end-user has been having, why he chose the product, and the end results of the purchase—savings in dollars, reduced man-hours, greater safety, etc. The article can be illustrated by photos, graphs, or drawings. If it is written by a publication staff member, his or her by-line should be provided. If it is written by a company PR writer, the by-line should be omitted. After all, a company by-line would suggest that the company is merely tooting its own horn.

If the product is one that sells to the consumer through the retailer, the case-history should be slightly different. Instead of having as its locale an industrial site, it should take place in some appropriate kind of store—hardware, discount, paint, furniture, clothing, etc., and the article should be written for a national or regional publication whose readers are retailers, rather than industrial end-users. It should address goals meaningful to a retailer, such as more profits per square foot, greater traffic, better point-of-purchase display, and innovative sales techniques. Regardless of what the article is about, it is usually most credible when it refers only indirectly to the product that the company is selling. In spite of the indirectness, the article shows readers of the publication that other stores are stocking the product—in other words, that there *is* a demand for it.

The case history is a potent way of establishing that the product is being sold—in spite of what competition is saying about it. Merchandising the case-history article after it appears, in the form of a reprint, obtains still further exposure for it.

PROOF POSITIVE

Another way to demonstrate consumer satisfaction with the product—without raising the credibility issue—is to conduct a focus-group study and then publicize the results. A focus group consists of a number of people selected at random from, say, shoppers at a shopping center, respondents to an ad for participants in the study, actual users of the product (industrial or consumer), industrial authorities or end-users, or some related professional groups. Such a study usually consists of exposing samples of the product to members of the group and noting their reactions —on videotape or by means of filled-in questionnaires. One dentist I know was asked regularly to visit a local center, work on patients with a variety of products, and comment on his reactions to the products—pro or con. His reactions became part of a statistical study that included the reactions of other dentists who participated in a similar way. The same generally holds for other types of focus-group studies. The statistics generated by the study can be publicized through news releases, feature articles, and papers read at seminars, with reprints of the resulting publicity merchandised by the sales organization.

The same approaches—case histories or focus-group studies —can be used to show positive evidence that what competition might be saying about the product is not true. That applies whether competition's no-demand argument is directed at product quality, utility, uniqueness, or price. Naturally, you needn't limit your VR approaches to those cited here. These are just some examples of how to discredit in a dramatic way the no-demand ploy being used by your competition. A little thought should allow you to come up with a number of other effective techniques. There is no reason for you not to employ them all at the same time or consecutively. The more you do to disprove the negative rumors about your company or product, the better off you are.

DEMONSTRATING COMMITMENT

In this discussion of no-demand vulnerability, we touched briefly on another type: the "lack-of-commitment" vulnerability. We recall that competitors of the photo-equipment company—who were established in the new markets the company was exploring— claimed that this sudden interest would disappear after conditions righted themselves in the company's primary industry. What they were really saying was that the photo-equipment manufacturer had no lasting commitment to the new markets. Competition was, in fact, using this lack-of-commitment argument as a type of marketing strategy, which it hoped might keep prospective customers from straying into the clutches of the newcomer.

A similar lack-of-commitment vulnerability can be seen in a totally different industry. A major manufacturer had been producing electronic chips for use in its own product line. At one point, the company announced its decision to market the chips to other firms, as well. The decision was undoubtedly a wise one because it allowed the company to increase production, thereby reducing the cost per chip, and to open markets for itself in other industries. As wise as the decision was, however, it was not risk-free. Competition is constantly alert to any incursion into its markets and tries to find ways of stopping it. Anyone not realizing this is in for trouble. In the case cited here, competition attempted to make prospective customers believe that the electronic chip manufacturer was merely trying to get rid of overcapacity during a lull in sales for its main product line in which the chip was used. In effect, what they were saying was that once sales picked up in the manufacturer's primary field, the chips would no longer be available from that supplier, who would be making them exclusively for his own products. In short, it was alleged, he had a lack of commitment.

The way to counter such statements made by competition is to demonstrate as visibly as possible that the company is in the new industry for keeps.

One way of demonstrating commitment to an industry is to establish a scholarship fund for students interested in entering the field. Publicizing it at every turn would gain the exposure needed to help convince prospective customers of the company's commitment. This involves publicizing the establishment of the scholarship, how candidates are being screened for it, who has been appointed to the screening committee, and, finally, the awarding of the scholarship to the winner. That final stage might be accompanied by considerable fanfare—possibly a dinner, speeches, invited notables from the industry, and so on. An event such as this, staged annually (and designated at the outset as the first annual scholarship award) can go a long way toward disproving what competition is saying—that the company has no long-lasting commitment to the industry.

There are other ways to demonstrate commitment, too. Like anything else in PR (or VR), discovering them calls for little more than exercising one's creative powers.

More Vulnerabilities

Don't think for a moment that the few vulnerability situations we've discussed cover them all. Discovering vulnerabilities is a little like digging a hole. The more you dig, the more dirt you find to shovel. There are vulnerabilities that cover virtually every facet of business, from manufacturing to marketing, including service, maintenance, and financing. Each one offers competition an opportunity to gain an advantage.

Ten Common Vulnerabilities

Following is a brief description of ten common vulnerabilities. Finding ways to deal with them will be up to you. Bear in mind, though, that the list just barely scratches the surface.

1. The "inadequate-warrantee" vulnerability has become a powerful marketing tool for automobile manufacturers. In fact, sometimes they engage in warrantee wars—vaunting their own warrantees and knocking those of their competitors. In such cases, automakers state their arguments loud and clear. But in other industries—electronic and hi-fi equipment and appliances, for example—manufacturers are less outspoken about their warrantees, the terms of which are rarely read by a customer until after he has purchased the product and needs to have it repaired. Then he discovers that the warrantee, good for only 90 days, has long since expired. Couple a short-term warrantee with a product that is rumored to have a high failure rate and you have the makings of a

vulnerability situation that a competitor's salespeople can play to the hilt.

2. In marketing, the "sins of the parent" are often visited on the children as a form of vulnerability. In many instances, the children are undeserving of the stigma. This generally happens when the product of a parent company is found wanting. Then products produced by the company's divisions and subsidiaries may fall prey to the same image, whether they deserve it or not. In spite of that, many marketing people continue on their merry way, without altering their strategies, while their parent companies are being attacked for one reason or another, often with some validity. What they are overlooking is that competition is not sitting by and letting the parent's problem go unnoticed in the division's marketing arena. In fact, competition is probably busy making certain that prospective customers know about the parent company's problem and its possible impact on divisions and subsidiaries.

3. The "not-local" vulnerability is, in reality, a scare tactic. It was used years ago in the grocery field, when local independent grocers spread the word that food chains and supermarkets, with their parent companies located elsewhere, were taking money out of the community. This, they claimed, harmed the community. The same argument is often used today against national corporations who compete in a community against regional or local businesses. My national security guard client encountered a somewhat different version of this problem. Its local offices were said not to have as intimate a knowledge of the community's security needs as a local company did. These kinds of allegations, repeated frequently enough and with conviction, can carry a good deal of weight in a competitive marketing situation.

4. The "trade-show" vulnerability is one that many established companies face. It is the reason that companies reserve booth space even though they doubt that being an exhibitor at a particular trade show is worthwhile. They are afraid not to. Why? Because they fear they will be noted for their absence. It isn't hard to believe the charge that a company is not exhibiting at a popular trade show because it is doing poorly and is therefore cutting expenses. This is particularly true if the company has previously been a regular exhibitor at a particular show. Companies are frequently in such fear of this vulnerability that in order to put in an

appearance at a trade show they skimp in other—often more vital —marketing areas.

5. The "imminent-takeover" vulnerability (discussed earlier) affects a company in two ways. Because of internal uncertainties arising from the situation, management is unable to respond to changing marketing conditions. Often, it is so preoccupied with the takeover that it lacks the time for or interest in analyzing and acting on competitive marketing threats. Also, if the takeover is about to occur or has just occurred, marketing executives are not quite sure how the new management would like them to react. So nothing happens—and whatever competition says or does remains uncontested.

This vulnerability also manifests itself externally. Think of what your competitors' salespeople can say when your company is on the verge of a takeover—or rumored to be: That your product lines might be discontinued; your sales policies might be changed; your interest in certain markets might wane; your maintenance and servicing policies might be affected to the detriment of the customer; your pricing might not be as attractive after the takeover; your suppliers might be changed, affecting product quality; and so on. Obviously, competition has a lot of ammunition to work with when a takeover (or merger) may be in the offing. It is important for a company's marketing executives to realize this and set counter-activities in motion as protective measures during this uncertain interim period.

6. The "labor-unrest" vulnerability can be a rumored situation that may never come to pass. Yet, competition can use it as a scare tactic with prospective customers. For example, should an OEM be considering a long-term purchase of your product as a component of its own product, the prospect of a strike could easily upset the sale. The reason is that the item might become unavailable and affect the customer's production and marketing of its own product. A rumored strike might also throw a monkey wrench into financing that the company might be arranging with banks or private investors. And an awareness of this financing problem gives potential customers another reason to be wary of doing business with the company. They might be fearful that the problem will affect production of the item they would be purchasing.

Suppliers, too, are sensitive about doing business with a company when a strike seems imminent. The supplier, which may have a choice of companies it can sell its product to, may be hesitant about an alliance with a company that may soon stop ordering because of a labor-caused shutdown—especially when the supplier's own products may be in limited supply. In that case, the vendor would rather target its sales at customers who represent a stable and uninterrupted flow of orders. Meanwhile, customers of the strike-threatened company realize that the company may be unable to continue production—at least at current prices or quantities—because vendors may opt not to sell it. Thus, a company threatened with a strike, or rumored to be, can find itself in a vise-like situation—squeezed on all sides.

7. The "product-failure" vulnerability is an age-old one. Nevertheless, it manages to frighten away potential customers for a company's products. Two of my clients—one a hi-fi equipment manufacturer and the other a computer terminal manufacturer— faced such a problem. Both were seriously affected by it, so much so that one redesigned its line and the other spent heavily on revamping its manufacturing facilities. Whether their equipment failures were real, existed to some small degree, or were merely ugly rumors spread by competition, the result was the same. The companies were faced with a loss of business that had to be restored—or else. Don't think that such a situation doesn't start a competitor's sales staff drooling over the possibilities.

8. Akin to the previous vulnerability is the "poor-quality-control" vulnerability. This may be very impersonal, relating only to product, or it may relate to specific quality–control executives within a company. It may originate with a rumor that the company is buying components for its product line from second-rate companies that exercise little quality control. Or it may reflect on the company's own manufacturing facilities or its quality control procedures. The problem can exist whether a company is selling to industrial end-users or OEMs or through retailers to the consumer.

In each instance, customers will be wary about purchasing the company's products. And the stigma causing that wariness can hurt a firm for a long, long time. It is far from unheard of for a company to have a reputation for producing second-rate products —worth purchasing only if they are inexpensive and certainly not meriting the fancy price tags of top-of-the-line products. Such a reputation even affects the caliber of the rep, distributor, or retailer that will carry the line. With the ripples so widespread, it is a little frightening to think that such an image may have little or no basis in fact—initiated, perhaps, by a jealous competitor.

9. Even "inadequate packaging" can represent a serious vulnerability. I mention this to emphasize that virtually any area, regardless of how inconsequential it may seem, can turn into a vulnerability affecting a company's sales potential. In this case, the vulnerability can stem from the external appearance of the packaging or from the physical structure of the package.

As we know, packaging has become an integral part of retail point-of-purchase selling. The more attractive, more informative package stands a greater chance of catching the consumer's attention. Realizing that, the retailer is more apt to give greater shelf space to the well-designed package. Economical-looking packaging, even though the product inside may be of superior quality, tends to make the consumer doubt the quality of the merchandise. And competition can take advantage of that—even when its own product is inferior. Its salespeople can sell the retailer on the importance of good packaging, while demeaning the other company's packaging.

The physical protection that packaging affords a product can also be an area of vulnerability. Many companies have carried structural package design to the level of a science. But others continue to package and ship products in makeshift, noncustomized enclosures. In the first instance, products are well protected and usually arrive safely, undamaged. In the latter case, the shipping of products from the manufacturer to the distributor, the retailer, or the end-user may contribute to the product's demise long before it gets put to use. Distributors or retailers, who shelf-stock packaged products in vast quantities, are continually alert to shoddily packaged merchandise. They fear that customers receiving damaged goods will blame it on them. Because the risk of inheriting such an image is too great, many are careful to inventory only well-packaged products. Any hint that a company may not protect its products adequately is a strong reason not to do business with that company. The hint may come from the retailer's or distributor's peer groups at trade-show get-togethers or from other companies' salespeople, who find this one more opportunity to toss a few daggers at the competition.

10. The "warehousing" vulnerability is one that must be familiar to everyone in marketing. It affects the price of a product and the speed of response in getting the product to whomever requests it. Basically, it has to do with the proximity of a warehouse—whether it is or isn't near the customer. If it isn't, the cost of shipping over great distances to deliver an order may price the product out of the market. Also, the time required to ship a vital product to a company in need of it might be too long. Take a newspaper in need of a replacement part for its press in time for its next edition. Parts warehoused too far away might not arrive in time. In such a case, it is better to do business with a company whose warehouses are nearby. These are important considerations in dealing with a company. As such, they provide excellent material for competition to use when the selling gets a little rough.

There are many more vulnerabilities than the ten noted here. One major company, for example, was even attacked for being in league with the Devil because of the design of its trademark. According to the press, the charge may have originated with distributors of competing products. It doesn't take much imagination for competition to come up with vulnerabilities that can be pinned to your company. But it does take a good deal of imagination to undo them.

Once You've Got It, Keep It

As a parting shot, we ought to examine a few of the things that tend to negate PR and VR efforts. These include ways to alienate editorial people and ways to detract from the credibility of PR placements that *do* appear in a publication.

BUYING EDITORIAL

Perhaps one of the worst practices that companies are sometimes guilty of is intimidating the space salesman—the media rep who sells you advertising space in a publication (or time on TV or radio). In publications that have integrity and are striving for a leadership position with their target audiences, advertising and editorial are usually kept far apart from each other. In other words, even though the media rep's chances of selling space or time to a particular company may be increased by his attempt to influence the editorial staff to run something about the company, he cannot do it.

Still, time and again, advertisers ask their ad or PR agencies to exert pressure on the space rep. The request often comes in the form of a veiled threat to cancel an advertising schedule unless the medium runs editorial about the company. However, a publication or other medium worth its salt will generally turn its back on such proposals. The advertiser, in turn, ought to respect this policy and not attempt to violate it. In many instances, advertisers or their agents who pursue these strong-arm methods end up alienating the medium's editorial people. For the sake of appearances, the space rep might throw them a crumb every so often—possibly a 50-word mention and a photo of a new product. But that's about all. The effort won't result in feature articles about the company or inclusion of the company and its people in roundup articles or in the news section of the publication.

Of course, there are always some media that will trade PR exposure for advertising. These are usually not top-flight magazines, newspapers, or stations in their markets. And one of the reasons they aren't is that their audiences have lost respect for their editorial practices. We watch TV or read publications because we expect to come away with something we didn't know before. When we begin seeing editorial about companies or products that are advertising regularly in the same medium, we begin to suspect that the editorial staff is not trying to benefit the reader, but trying to please the advertiser. At that point, the medium's editorial loses its credibility and begins to resemble propaganda. That is when an audience stops believing in the editorial and eventually stops reading the publication or watching the station.

The point applies to some magazines despite their impressive circulation figures. How do they manage to lose credibility but keep readers? In fact, they don't. Readers receive many publications in the mail *free*. When the magazines are reputable, recipients look forward to reading the editorial. Otherwise they ignore them or throw them away. They don't read the editorial and wouldn't pay for the opportunity—if they had to.

Many trade, industrial, and business publications do not require paid subscriptions from their readers. They obtain their revenue chiefly from advertising. Nevertheless, they are excellent publications and regularly screen their readers before putting them on their mailing list. These publications shouldn't be classified as propaganda-type magazines just because they are circulated for free. But some free publications are of the propaganda type. And they should be avoided. When a publication is ready, even eager, to trade editorial space for advertising space, you can assume that the editorial bonus your company will receive will have little or no value. Since the publication lacks credibility with its audience, who will believe the publicity—or, for that matter, read it?

SEPARATING EDITORIAL AND ADVERTISING

Another mistake that tends to negate the value of editorial exposure is placing a PR story about a company or product alongside an ad for the company or product. This happens to be a practice of many advertisers. Apparently, they believe that the reader will be impressed with their clout in getting editorial along with the advertising. And many publications like to cater to their advertisers in this fashion—even the nonpropaganda types that may just *happen* to have editorial about the company or product in the same issue as the ad. Why not put them together, you ask? Well, even appearing in the same issue, no less on an adjacent page, is bad practice. It triggers the reader's sixth sense. He begins to suspect that there might have been some dirty work afoot— that the editorial was, in reality, traded for the advertising space and, as such, is nothing more than company-paid propaganda.

However, there is one situation when the simultaneous appearance of editorial and advertising for a company needn't reflect badly on either the company or the publication. It might have come about purely through the efforts of the space rep, who should continually be watching for opportunities to sell space. When he spots in his publication's editorial calendar that an article about a particular product, product category, or industry will be appearing in the March issue, he should make every effort to sell space in that issue to relevant companies. It makes good sense. And it's not bad practice for the advertiser to appear in an issue that includes mention of his company or product among mentions of similar companies or products (e.g., in a roundup article)—just as long as the article isn't solely about his company or product. If it were, it would come off as propaganda. In that case, it is often preferable to reschedule the ad for a different issue. If that is impossible, then try to get the ad and editorial as many pages from each other as you can.

HOLDING PRESS CONFERENCES

PR professionals must also develop strong resistance to their client's or company's penchant for press conferences. In my own experience, companies are apt to call one—at the drop of a hat. It might be to announce a new product line, a new advertising thrust, new executives, a new plant or headquarters location, or new production facilities. Often, the news really does warrant a press conference. But public relations people should be aware that companies often consider "PR" short for press conference and believe that such events are the PR professional's primary function. However, that is not necessarily true—most of the time. And PR people shouldn't be too eager to jump at the chance of staging a press conference whenever the company or client wants one. It can sometimes do a company a lot of harm in terms of relationships with the editorial world. Editors are constantly faced with deadlines and the need to grind out volumes of material by deadline time. Leaving their desks to attend an event not only takes time, but makes meeting deadlines even tougher.

When the subject matter is truly "hot" and warrants press-conference treatment, then the editor is pleased to have been invited and feels even more kindly towards the company and its PR people (particularly when those people have taken the trouble to find out when that publication's editorial deadline is and schedule the press conference for some other time, if at all possible).

But when an editor gets the feeling he has wasted time that could have been better spent behind a typewriter, then watch out. He may be "out to lunch" the next time you approach him with a story idea or another invitation.

How can we decide what subject matter justifies holding a press conference? Sometimes, it's not easy. Generally, however, we can decide by asking ourselves this question: Could the same information be given to an editor by visiting him at his office or by mailing him material and discussing it with him over the phone?

The way to answer that question is by determining if some significant aspect of the material would be lost through a PR person's office visit or by mail/phone treatment. Usually the answer is in favor of the press conference when two criteria are met: When equipment has to be seen in operation in order to be understood and appreciated and when certain people—company executives, engineers, scientists, and so on—must be on hand for answering technical or complex questions asked by the media. Normally, everything else can be handled by visiting an editor at his office— everything except a vital equipment demonstration and an equally vital question-and-answer period. If those two requirements must be met—or else the media will miss what is truly important about the announcement—then a press conference is justified. If not, don't risk alienating editors, whose friendships you will be counting on at some later date. Of course, even if the two criteria are met, a press conference may not be absolutely necessary. You must ask yourself if the risk is worth it.

Although the next point has been mentioned briefly before, it is so important that it is worth bringing up again.

FOLLOWING UP

A call to an editor following the mailing of a news release is not worth the future grief that may come from it. If you've ever visited an editorial office, you've probably noticed one thing common to them all: An enormous stack of press releases. Usually the stack is scattered all over the editor's desk and even heaped on other surfaces around his office. Many of the releases may have arrived by mail or messenger that very day. Believe me, going through them is a tedious, time-consuming task that is spliced in with banging out editorial material on the typewriter. Getting a phone call in the midst of all this, the editor is not likely to be in the most receptive frame of mind.

Of course, the editor won't object if the call tips him off to something valuable—possibly a scoop or exclusive on something newsworthy going on in the industry. However, when that call is from someone asking him if he has received a press release and intends to use it—followed, possibly, by a fast sales pitch on why the information is "vital" and ought to be used—then the editor begins to feel that he is being taken advantage of. He is.

No PR professional will want to establish that kind of image with editors, particularly those he intends to work with and send releases to regularly. It is an image that can only hurt him and his clients or company. The best approach is not to hang everything on the appearance in print of any particular release. The PR professional should, instead, be grinding out releases on a steady basis so that, by the law of averages, some ought to make it on their own—without a follow-up call.

USING REPRINTS

A final note—this time on what not to do with PR *after* it has gotten its exposure. It has to do with the format of the reprint, mentioned earlier in passing. The credibility of an article reprint depends on its link to the magazine that published it. Many companies stretch that link to its breaking point, treating the reprint like a company brochure, with advertising messages, slogans, logos, listings of reps, distributors, warehouses, phone numbers, and addresses. Doctored in this manner, the reprint no longer smacks of editorial. It looks more like company-inspired literature. The credibility of third-party endorsement is all but lost.

To preserve the third-party endorsement, companies should exercise restraint in their editorial reprints, giving them the appearance of material that the magazine itself might have sent to its readers. Reproducing the cover of the magazine on the front of the reprint helps establish that. Reproducing the cover in full color, if it was originally printed that way, helps establish the editorial image even more. Omitting a company's name, address, logo, and phone number from the white space surrounding the article is extremely hard to do. But if a reprint is to realize its full potential as editorial, then the company ought to resist the temptation and avoid cluttering it with elements that detract from its credibility. A business card attached to the reprint will serve the same purpose— only more effectively.

After all, credibility is what PR is all about. Lose it and you've lost the battle.

Index

TITLES OF INTEREST IN
PRINT AND BROADCAST MEDIA

For further information or a current catalog, write:
NTC Business Books
a division of *NTC Publishing Group*
4255 West Touhy Avenue
Lincolnwood, Illinois 60646-1975 U.S.A.
800-323-4900 (in Illinois, 708-679-5500)